C4

THE WAITER

The Restaurateur's Guide to
Guéridon and Lamp Cookery

The Chef's Manual of Kitchen Management

The Caterer's Potato Manual

Hotel Keeping and Catering as a Career

The Chef's Compendium of Professional Recipes
(with E. Renold)

Catering Management in the Technological Age (Ed.)

The Waiter

Originally edited by A. C. Marshall

Revised as a

NEW AND AUGMENTED EDITION

by

JOHN FULLER

Rank Organisation Professor of Hotel Management
Director, The Scottish Hotel School
The University of Strathclyde

and

A. J. CURRIE

Assistant Chief Waiting Examiner
The Hotel and Catering Institute

BARRIE AND JENKINS
LONDON

MADE AND PRINTED IN GREAT BRITAIN BY
THE GARDEN CITY PRESS LIMITED
LETCHWORTH, HERTFORDSHIRE

Contents

Illustrations

Charts and Diagrams

Preface

The first edition of *The Waiter* was published in 1947 for the former National Council for Hotel and Catering Education. It was edited by A. C. Marshall, for many years Headmaster of Westminster Technical College's hotel school, in collaboration with the chosen representatives of all the recognised organisations in the hotel and catering industry. It has been a standard text-book for waiting staff and hotel and catering students ever since.

In 1960, a revised edition was produced under the direction of The Hotel and Catering Institute, whose education committee had taken over many of the functions of the former National Council. That edition was edited by the noted hotelier, O. G. Goring, a past Chairman of The Hotel and Catering Institute and N. L. W. Barratt, the Institute's Chief Examiner in Waiting. *The Waiter* owes much to the original editor and revisers to whom we acknowledge indebtedness. At the same time, we stress that the former contributors and editors are in no way responsible for any defects in the new version which this foreword introduces.

In this present edition, the contributions of the original compilers and subsequent revisers have substantially been preserved, though much material has been re-arranged and consolidated. Further, the opportunity has been taken to expand the text to meet more closely the needs of students preparing for today's catering examinations and to include additional material useful for waiters (or waitresses) during the early years of training and experience. The result is a new and larger version of *The Waiter*.

As a matter of policy, The Hotel and Catering Institute, now functioning purely as the professional body for qualified hoteliers and caterers, no longer sponsors this or any other text book, but we have kept in mind, and have endeavoured to meet, the aims which first prompted the establishment of their Universal Catering Primers of which *The Waiter* was the first, namely "to provide the basis of teaching in all official training schemes now in operation".

JOHN FULLER

A. J. CURRIE

Glasgow 1965

1

The Waiter's Role in Catering

In the social and economic conditions of today, more and more people eat away from home. Thus, there can be few who do not have a general notion of the work of the waiter and waitress and its broad purpose. Nevertheless, it is worth noting that those with responsibilities for the service of food have a vital role in hotel keeping and catering, Britain's fourth biggest industry in terms of numbers employed, and one which helps substantially to support the tourist and travel industry as the country's top earner of foreign currency. Good waiters are necessary to the success and development of this important tourist, hotel and catering industry, to business as well as holiday travel and, hence, to the well-being of society and its economic strength.

Waiting staff in the catering industry are an important link in the chain of food production and selling which can be summarised as:

A. food is grown by farmers, then
B. shipped or transported to markets, to be
C. sold by wholesalers to caterers who
D. prepare, cook and serve it to the public.

The charts on pages 4 and 6 further illustrate the nature of catering and the waiter's part in it.

The waiter not only serves food, but does, as the following

chapters show, play an important part as, in effect, a salesman of food—one who assists materially in merchandising—and its accompanying services. Waiters and waitresses are really "sales staff" in a firm, just as the chef is its manufacturer, turning raw materials into palatable dishes.

A successful hotel, restaurant or cafe is one which guests are anxious to visit again, a place where they feel as comfortable as in their own homes. This pleasant atmosphere is produced by courtesy; good, well-cooked food; advice in selecting from the available dishes; a knowledge of how they are prepared; and quiet, efficient, but unostentatious, service. It is by these amenities that both buyer and seller are satisfied and goodwill of the business increased.

THE PARTNERS. A successful catering establishment depends on three partners—management, cooks and sales staff. They have different parts to play, but they belong to a united team. All must have an interest in the work, a feeling of pride in the concern and a sense of loyalty towards it. With this attitude of mind, there is no drudgery in any of the work.

One attraction of the catering industry is that, at a time when so many jobs are growing increasingly monotonous and packed with the same deadening routine throughout the year, it offers a career full of interest and variety. The sales staff—waiters, for example—come into contact with a wide range of people, all with different interests; they are consequently prompted to develop tact and initiative and, by keeping their brains active, reveal their personality.

Because the waiter is in direct contact with guests, he must be regarded in many situations as representing the owners of the hotel or restaurant in which he works. He thus contributes generally (or the reverse) to the good image and repute of the establishment employing him.

Much of catering and hotel-keeping's success, therefore, depends on the skills, interest and personal qualities of the waiter.

Moreover, waiting is not only important as a link in the chain of food preparation and service but as holding vast possibilities for the right person. In fact many of the best restaurant proprietors throughout the world started as junior waiters. It is also true to say that every restaurant manager in the world has had long actual experience in waiting; for without proper knowledge and skill based on such experience he could not hold the position he does. There is no short cut to restaurant management. One cannot just "drop into" this position. However, today especially it is well worth trying to start a steady climb to it because as is well known, the good restaurateur can command a high salary and enjoy a respected status in the community.

The efficiency of the waiter reacts upon the success of the hotel, restaurant or other catering establishment for which he is working. His work, his attitude to those above him and to his fellows, the way he deals with those who come to the restaurant, (who may be referred to as "guests", "customers", "patrons", or "visitors"), have their effect in building up the reputation of the establishment and thereby affect his own career. This applies also, of course, to waitresses. It may be taken that wherever the word waiter is used, it refers also to waitresses, unless it is stated otherwise.

Advancement

Nearly all posts of head waiter (or, of course, head waitress), maitre d'hôtel, or restaurant manager, are obtained by those who have spent years of service in waiting, and have learned, by training and experience, the best ways to do the work which they organise and direct. This applies, also, to

Nature and Structure of the Catering Industry

A. SUPPLIES OF MATERIALS USED IN CATERING
(Food, drink, tobacco, furniture, equipment, etc.),
Requiring the skill of:

Farmers, planters, market gardeners, fish trawling companies, and most types of
manufacturer.

THESE REQUIRE THE HELP OF

B. Importers, shipping companies, railway and road transport.

C. Manufacturers' agents, wholesale merchants and wholesale produce markets.

FOR SALE

D. (In the form of board and lodgings, or meals)
IN

Hotels, Inns and Steamships	Restaurants, Cafés, Snack Bars, etc.	Industrial and Staff Restaurants	Boarding Houses	Public Houses	Hospitals, Colleges, Schools

Which need approximately a total of 700,000 men and women staff of all kinds.

many of the most successful owners of catering establishments.

Good service is sought throughout the country, so that a good waiter has always a large number of opportunities for promotion.

Conditions of Work

As in all industries, Government Acts controlling hours, wages and conditions exist in the Catering Industry. Wages Boards* have been formed, so that minimum rates of pay (and other conditions of service) may be regulated for the various sections of the industry. It is, however, not desirable in this textbook to indicate what these regulations are, but the following statements should be taken as an indication of the conditions that apply in the industry generally.

The waiter is in the favoured position of spending the greater part of his time in the public rooms, which are well lighted, carpeted, clean and comfortable. Food has to be brought from the kitchen to the restaurant. Where there are service lifts, or the kitchen is on the same floor as the restaurant, service can be straightforward without strain to the staff. In many establishments the food has to be carried upstairs or downstairs, according to the kitchen lay-out.

The waiter is nearly always on his feet, for he has to stand or walk about for many hours daily.

The hours he will work vary according to the establishment. In a hotel that is open from early morning until late at night, the staff must be on duty (probably on "shifts") at all the times necessary to prepare for and serve the visitors. In canteens or restaurants run for business people, or in departmental stores and similar establishments, the hours will approximate to those of other callings, e.g., from 9.0

* Or Wages Councils.

Waiting in Various Types of Catering

HOTELS, INNS and STEAM-SHIPS	RESTAURANTS, CAFES, SNACK BARS etc.	INDUSTRIAL and STAFF RESTAURANTS	BOARDING HOUSES	PUBLIC HOUSES	HOSPITALS, COLLEGES, SCHOOLS
		FOOD IS BOUGHT BY The owners of the above catering establishments or their managers.			
		THEN PREPARED BY Cooks (varying from the chef de cuisine with his staff of 50 or more in a large hotel to the one cook of a small concern).			
		AND IS THEN SERVED BY WAITERS, AS FOLLOWS:			
Assistant waiters (called 'commis') under a waiter (called 'chef de rang'), under a Head Waiter or Maître d'Hôtel, with special waiters for wines, bars, lounges, banquets: all under a Restaurant Manager	(As in a hotel, except that many more waitresses than waiters are employed)	Waitresses under a Head Waitress, under a Manager or Manageress	Waitress under a Head Waitress under a Manager or Manageress	Bar Attendants (men and women)	Waitress under a Head Waitress, under a Catering Officer, Organizer or Housekeeper

a.m. to 6.0 p.m., with one half-day free on Saturday, and all Sunday free.

The remuneration of waiters has for many years been considerably above that obtainable in most comparable occupations. This remuneration may be in the form of a regular fixed amount, as in canteens, snack bars, etc., but in hotels and restaurants it is usually made up of a weekly guaranteed sum, with the addition of tips, which may be a share of all the tips paid to the staff or just what the waiter may himself receive from his customers. In addition, he nearly always has meals free, or under specially favourable staff arrangements.

He may be non-resident or resident. In the large hotels, nearly all the men live out, but about two-thirds of the women staff live in. In small hotels and boarding houses, the proportion of men and women living in is greater. Staffs of canteens, departmental stores, snack bars, day restaurants and cafés, mostly live out.

Restaurant Staff

The number of staff and the allocation of duties depends on the size and exclusiveness of the restaurant.

In a large restaurant, whether belonging to an hotel, a non-residential establishment or within industrial catering, there must be one person in charge. Under him or her there will be principal assistants in charge of sections of the room and under each of these will come the general assistants.

In a small restaurant the person in charge may be called Restaurant Manager, maître d'hôtel or head waiter, and his assistants may all be called "waiters".

In the largest and highest class establishments, waiting staff is still organised in the French restaurant system as a restaurant brigade. This organisation may be reduced or simplified but a classification of possible staff is as follows:

RESTAURANT MANAGER—DIRECTEUR DU RESTAURANT. He is responsible for all the restaurant service and is in general charge of all persons connected with it. He quotes prices for daily menus and, in addition, (unless there is a separate banqueting manager) makes arrangements for banquets and private parties.

HEAD WAITER OR MAÎTRE D'HÔTEL. He is in direct charge of either the whole of a small restaurant or part of a larger one. He supervises service, receives guests (either directly or from the restaurant manager) and seats them. He may take the orders from the guests and pass them to the station waiters. In large establishments there may be subordinate or assistant head waiters, i.e., second or third head waiters (deuxième or troisième maîtres d'hôtel) and/or a reception head waiter (maître d'hôtel de reception) to take 'phone bookings and enter them in the reservation book, and to receive guests and direct them to a table.

STATION HEAD WAITER—*Maitre d'hotel de Carré.* He is responsible for a section of the restaurant carrying out similar functions in his own area to those of the maître d'hôtel.

STATION WAITER—*Chef de Rang.* He is in charge of a *"rang"* or group of about 5 tables, to seat approximately 20 guests. He is responsible for taking guests' orders and for serving them, for the cleanliness of his *rang* or station and for ensuring the proper service of each dish in the right sequence.

JUNIOR STATION WAITER—*Demi Chef.* He has similar

duties to a station waiter but normally works a smaller station and often without the aid of assistants or commis.

ASSISTANT WAITER—*Commis Waiter*. There are several kinds of junior assistants known as commis. For example, assistant station waiter—commis de rang, assists the station waiter and is responsible for giving food checks into the kitchen, bringing dishes to side-tables, removing plates from guests tables and returning used plates and dishes to the service area and by generally attending on the station waiter. Commis de rang may also be known as commis de suite.

TROLLEY ASSISTANT WAITER—*Commis de wagon*. He is a commis, an assistant waiter, assigned to a trolley (a voiture or wagon) usually of hors d'oeuvres or pâtisserie.

CLEARING ASSISTANT WAITER—*Commis Debarasseur*. Is the most junior assistant, mainly clearing away used plates and dishes and simply "fetching and carrying" under instruction. He holds this post only during a short period of early training.

APPRENTICES—*Apprentis*. In apprenticeship, young waiters work up through the assistant posts. In Continental brigades young waiters or apprentices are known as piccolo (literally "little ones" from the Italian).

WINE BUTLER OR WINE WAITER—*Chef de vin* or *Sommelier*. Takes orders for wines, spirits, beers and soft drinks and serves them to guests. He, too, may have his own assistant wine waiter (commis de vin).

Additionally, big restaurants may have other specialist staff such as:

CARVER—*Trancheur* wearing either chef's dress or certainly white jacket and normally an apron.

SPECIAL TROLLEY SERVICE WAITERS. Such as costumed servers for Turkish coffee or Indian costumed attendants for the service of curries.

Ancillary Staff

RESTAURANT CASHIER. Sometimes the waiter is responsible for making out the bill and sometimes it is the responsibility of a cashier who is stationed either in a cash desk in the restaurant or in the service area.

In any case, the waiter presents the bill to the customer. (See Chapter 14).

2

Dress and Personal Factors in Waiting

The opening chapter stressed the importance of personal characteristics in discharging waiting duties, in "selling" and in guest contact. The following section indicates factors important in the personal development of the waiter.

Clothing

A waiter is usually required to wear some form of uniform.

Though traditional dress for the various grades has been indicated below, it should be noted that white jackets of varying patterns are increasingly worn by all ranks of waiting staff from chef de rang down. There is also increasing use of specially designed dress to conform with a restaurant's design and décor. Dress, for both men and women staff which can be laundered and thus frequently changed has obvious advantages from the point of view of hygiene and, when properly maintained, appearance also.

Traditional waiting dress, which also helps identify grades of staff is as follows:

RESTAURANT MANAGER—*Directeur du Restaurant.* He normally wears managerial dress, i.e., for day, morning clothes —black jacket (less frequently today the longer frock coat) and striped trousers and for evening—evening dress—of tails, white waistcoat and white tie; though in some (especially the smaller) establishments he might nowadays wear a dinner jacket.

HEAD WAITERS—*Maîtres d'hôtel.* Sometimes the premier maître d'hôtel (the first or *the* maître d'hôtel) is regarded as restaurant manager and wears managerial dress. Otherwise head waiters and subordinate maîtres d'hôtel normally wear: for evening (dinner)—tail coat, white waistcoat, wing collar and black bow tie; for day (luncheon)—tail coat, black waistcoat, wing collar and black bow tie.

STATION WAITERS—*Chefs de rang.* Tail coat, black waistcoat, wing collar, white bow tie.

JUNIOR STATION WAITERS—*Demi-Chefs.* Dress as for Chef de Rang.

ASSISTANT WAITERS—*Commis.* Wear black "café jacket" i.e., short, black jackets with accompanying black waistcoat, wing collar, white tie and long white aprons or alternatively (and today more frequently) white jackets in place of the black "café" jackets.

WINE WAITER—*Sommelier.* Traditional dress, either as a station waiter (though usually wearing lapel badges with grape design) or special black uniform with chain and cellar key and possibly black or green baize apron.

WAITRESSES. Traditional dress for waitresses is black or dark dress, with launderable collar, cuffs and cap (usually white) and apron (also usually white). Stockings and simple black shoes are worn. More and more establishments are, however, adopting distinctive uniform in both colour and design for waitresses.

RULES OF DRESS. Washable clothing should be frequently changed and worn freshly laundered. Suits (and for waitresses, dresses) must be kept well pressed and free from spots. Regular sponging is usually necessary to maintain and prolong smartness.

Shoes should be of conservative design and maintained clean, well polished and always in a good state of repair. Stockings or socks should be changed daily. Linen should be immaculately clean. Although the waiter is usually responsible for the supply and upkeep of his clothing it is customary for many hotels and restaurants to arrange at the establishment's cost, for the laundering of his linen.

Personal Qualities Required

Cleanliness

Because waiting staff deal with food, utmost cleanliness and good grooming is at all times necessary. This applies not only in high class hotels, but in every branch of catering, however humble customers may be. Guests are not likely to return to an establishment where they know the waiter or waitress is dirty.

FINGER NAILS AND HANDS. Must be washed frequently. Always wash immediately before service and always following use of the toilet. Nails and cuticles should be neatly trimmed and kept clean by use of the nail brush. Waitresses should avoid nail varnish whether clear or coloured when on duty. Smokers must ensure that they remove all traces of nicotine from fingers (pumice and bleach are useful).

BODILY CLEANLINESS. Cleanliness of the whole body is also essential; for any suggestion of odour or staleness is a most grave offence in a restaurant employee. A daily bath or shower should be the minimum standard for good waiting staff. Under clothing should be changed frequently. Talcum powder for body and feet is acceptable but scent (even for a waitress) must be avoided.

SKIN AND COMPLEXION. Clear skin and complexion depends on good health based on adequate exercise, sleep, diet and cleanly habits. Waiting staff should use their leisure for fresh air recreation and should try to ensure that wholesome fresh foods such as vegetables, fruit, wholemeal bread and milk are featured in their diet. Waitresses should use cosmetics sparingly and rarely—and only as consistent with a fresh appearance.

HAIR. Hair should be kept neatly trimmed and shampooed frequently to avoid dandruff and odour. Hair should be well brushed as well as combed. Men should avoid styles which cause hair to fall over the eyes; for tossing hair away from eyes especially by hand is offensive to guests during food service. Waitresses should adopt neat hair styles and particularly ensure a hair length which does not fall on to or below the collar.

TEETH. Teeth and a clean mouth are vital both for appearance and a wholesome breath. Teeth should be kept clean by brushing at least twice a day—certainly night and morning. Inspection by a dentist is advisable twice a year and certainly not less frequently than once a year. Dentures, if worn, must similarly be kept scrupulously clean.

FEET. Feet need care both for comfort and cleanliness. Keep toe nails trim and feet well washed. Corns and other painful blemishes may require treatment by a chiropodist; for more serious foot weakness medical advice should be sought. Socks or stockings should be changed and washed daily.

Shoes should be well fitting (with ample room for toe movement). Waitresses should avoid excessively high or pointed heels.

POSTURE. Good stance is also important for the appearance, comfort and efficiency of waiting staff. To stand upright and walk erect is to give a good impression to guests and also to avoid the bodily stresses that accompany slouching.

Waitresses are advised to wear sound quality and properly fitting foundation garments to aid posture and health as well as appearance.

Speech

A respectful manner towards customers is desirable. A waiter should never be servile, for he should be proud of his skill, particularly if he is a good waiter; but he is a technical salesman of his establishment and a good salesman should aim to please.

His voice should be clear, low in pitch and somewhat formal. He should be able to pronounce words properly and to express his ideas easily. Although he does not have to converse with customers, he should acquire a sound knowledge of good English, for the customers always like to hear a well-modulated, pleasing voice, with well-expressed answers to any questions they may ask.

A knowledge of a second language is of great help, particularly to waiters who seek service in the large London hotels or restaurants, where there are often foreign visitors. French is perhaps the most useful, for not only are menus often written in French, but it is the language used in cookery books and in repertoires of dishes based on "la cuisine française".

Courtesy

It is the hallmark of a good waiter to be courteous on all
occasions. He will certainly be courteous to the customer,
but should carry these good manners through to the service
room and the locker room. His manners should not be just
a part of the "technique of the restaurant", but inherent in
his nature and a sign of well-bred desire to please those with
whom he comes into contact.

Every customer, irrespective of his financial standing,
should be treated alike. There should never be any fawning
on those who may tip lavishly. Tips should be acknowledged
graciously: if placed on the table they should not be removed
until the customer has left.

Often the waiter must go out of his way to be considerate
or forbearing to a critical or ill-tempered person.

He should not pass in front of a customer, and at all times
give right of way to a guest. When not working he should
stand upright (with the waiter's cloth on his left arm); when
being spoken to he should stand erect and steady.

Honesty

Should be most strictly observed. Some waiters fall into
habits that are in fact dishonest, such as taking food from
the restaurant for consumption elsewhere in the establishment or at home, "borrowing" silver or linen for similar
purposes. These are a form of stealing and certainly denote,
at the very least, that the waiter has not acquired a true
professional attitude to his work.

He should take the greatest care of all equipment belonging to the establishment and never think that he can deal
with it wastefully or carelessly because it is not his own.

Co-operation

Since the success of the establishment depends on the proper co-ordination of all the staff, the waiter should aim to help his fellow-workers. This implies such conduct as not being jealous if another waiter has customers who pay higher tips, taking the proper turn in the queue in the kitchen for service, learning and keeping to the "rules of the house" in spirit as well as in the letter.

The locker room can be an orderly place if each waiter keeps all his articles in his own locker and puts any unwanted paper, cloths, cigarette-ends, etc., in the proper receptacles.

If a mistake should be made by his head waiter or by his assistant, a waiter should never remonstrate with or criticise him in the restaurant. First of all he should remedy the fault (e.g., bring the customer the dish that he states he ordered). Any explanation that may be necessary to prevent the error occurring again, or to apportion the blame for it, should be made outside the restaurant, preferably at the end of the service.

If the waiter studies their preferences (even their "fads") he will find that his customers will be delighted when they realise that their wishes are known and anticipated.

Technical Skill

The following chapters give details of the skill and knowledge that the waiter needs:

(a) Knowledge of the catering trade, of which he is an important member (Chapter 1).

(b) Knowledge of the foods that he will serve, menus, cooking-times, etc. (Chapters 4 and 5).

(c) Lay-out of the restaurant, canteen, etc., and their preparation for the service (Chapters 3, 6, 7 and 15).

(d) Actual method of serving, e.g., generally, on the floors, lounges, etc., or in canteens and bars (Chapters 8, 9, 10, 11, 12, 13, 15).

(e) Service of tobacco, cigarettes, cigars, etc. (Chapter 13).

(f) Service of wines, spirits, etc. (Chapter 13).

(g) A good groundwork (which may be classified as a sound general education and attitude to his career), and such special qualifications as ability to speak a foreign language or understand the customary French terms used in catering (Chapters 4 and 5).

(h) A number of special points that are emphasised at the end of this Chapter on pages 19 and 20.

Conduct in the Restaurant

When not serving, a waiter should stand by his station sideboard, his service cloth folded on to his left forearm. This applies whether there are customers on his station or not. He must never lean against walls or furniture.

A waiter must not converse, far less argue, with other members of the staff and emphatically never argue with guests. If a customer enters in conversation with a waiter, the latter must answer politely and as briefly as possible. The waiter should ask to be excused at the first opportunity, but he must use tact to avoid offending. A waiter must never start a conversation with guests. Except, possibly, on first welcoming he should not address guests as Mr. or Mrs. but always as "Sir" or "Madam". He never discusses other guests with his customers nor must he give information regarding guests. A waiter must discipline himself not to listen to guests' conversation, whether it is carried out loudly enough for him to hear or not. If he has any complaints to make to head waiter or to colleagues, a waiter must wait until service is over.

The waiter must never eat on duty and this includes chewing gum. He must never use bad language either in the restaurant or in the dressing room.

A waiter should avoid airs and mannerisms, but he can certainly cultivate his personality. This is particularly important for a head waiter. Reading and interest in affairs of the day, sport and constructive recreations can help here.

The waiter should be proud of his work and not treat it as an ordeal. He must always be in good humour, pleasing and obliging to the customers without being servile.

He must never indulge in preferential treatment of customers according to or in anticipation of the amount of tips he receives from them.

Causes of Offence

Bear in mind always, therefore, the positive qualities and skills to cultivate as outlined in the foregoing. Check, too, that you do not cause offence by lapses listed below.

Waiting Staff Offend If—

They forget to say "Thank you" or fail to acknowledge a tip.
They cadge for tips, count tips or jingle coins in their pockets.
They are bad tempered or indifferent.
They talk too much to table guests when guests are talking to each other—(in other words they are tactless).
They ignore guests by talking among themselves.
They hurry customers to get their "stations" clear in order that they can leave early.
They have a bad form of speech.
They by bad service (usually on the wrong side of the diner) spill soup or other foods.

They add up bills wrongly (against the customer)—this is
   dishonest.

They eat during the service.

They put service cloths in their trousers pockets or under
   the arm.

They soil menus by keeping them in their shirt fronts.

They carry pencils behind their ears or in their hair.

They have bad breath.

They have body odour.

They have unpleasant foot smell.

They have dirty or untidy hair.

They have dirty hands and finger nails.

They chew gum. In Britain it is taboo.

They have spotted or greasy clothes.

They fuss with hair or pick facial or skin blemishes.

They sneeze or cough carelessly (ensure this is done into a
   handkerchief but otherwise avoid using handkerchiefs "in
   the room" unless absolutely necessary.

They have dirty cuffs or shirt fronts (waiters).

They have dirty aprons or hair bands (waitresses).

They have unpolished shoes.

They wear high-heeled or otherwise unsuitable shoes.

They wear soiled or laddered stockings.

They wear jewellery (wedding rings and watches allowed).

They are bad timekeepers.

They quarrel or are noisy on duty.

They shirk their allotted responsibilities.

See how many of these faults you notice when *you* are a
customer. By avoiding these faults you will not only please
your customers and satisfy your employer, but will pave the
way to your promotion.

Applying for a Post

Personal factors and good manners are especially important when applying for employment. There is always a need for good waiters but, in attending for interview, the waiter is reminded to:

1. Be well-groomed, and quietly dressed.
2. Call between meal hours: 10.0 a.m. is an excellent time.
3. Use the service entrance.
4. Take his testimonials with him.
5. Take with him any insurance cards, etc., that will be needed if he obtains the post.

At the interview, he will find out the conditions of the post (wages, "live-in", or "live-out", etc.).

If he is applying in writing, he should state briefly, in ordinary good English, the position for which he is applying, the experience he has had and the names of those who have given him a testimonial or to whom reference may be made. If no indication has been given of the wages offered, he should state the wages he requires.

Apprenticeship

Boys and girls wishing to make a start in the vocation of waiter should note that there is a national apprenticeship scheme. Their local youth employment officer will have information about this. Otherwise enquiries may be made to The Secretary, National Joint Apprenticeship Council for the Hotel and Catering Industry, 191 Trinity Road, London, S.W.17.

3

The Restaurant and its Equipment

Although the efficiency of the waiter depends partly on his work behind the scenes, it is in the restaurant itself during the time that meals are served that the real test of his efficiency is made.

The term "restaurant" refers to:

1. The restaurant or grill room of a large residential hotel. Most probably it will be licensed. Entertainments, an orchestra, dancing, may be provided. (See Plate I).

2. The dining room of a smaller residential hotel, inn or boarding house, licensed or unlicensed.

3. A restaurant, licensed or unlicensed, catering for non-residents. This may vary from those which cater for wealthy patrons, offer a wide choice of dishes and are open until late at night, to those which offer a small choice of dishes (most probably "English fare") during business hours.

4. A café, tea-room, etc., where lighter meals are served. These are often under individual ownership, but include many run by companies owning a large number of identical establishments.

5. Industrial and staff restaurants, serving from a small number up to several thousand employees daily. These aim to provide employees with a choice of dishes which

I. The Restaurant

In a training restaurant, the student serving soup is wearing a white jacket with "patrol" collar—ideal dress for cleanliness and appearance. The students in the background (also on practical hotel "lab." exercises) are also wearing functional and attractive dress as waitress and wine butler.

II. A Character Restaurant

Today's version of the traditional "grill room" or "buttery"
is often a speciality or "theme" restaurant as is the Hilton
Hotel's London Tavern. Note that waiters' dress is in special
styling and fits the mood and character of the operation.

can be prepared in large quantities. If the customers "help themselves" at a service counter, the work of the staff is correspondingly reduced.

6. Snack bars (licensed or unlicensed) which specialise in quick service. These generally offer a variety of drinks, sandwiches, and quickly prepared dishes.

Furniture and Equipment

In all these establishments, the waiter will have charge of a large amount of furniture and equipment which must be ready for service as required. He should know how to keep them in good condition, clean, properly laid out and ready for service.

Furniture will naturally vary according to the nature of the establishment. Floors may be covered with costly carpeting, polished wood or even, in simpler restaurants, in linoleum or plastic floor covering. Chairs similarly vary in upholstery and covering according to the degree of luxury sought. Curtains, other drapes, table lamp and other light fittings and so on are similarly highly variable in quality and design. The waiter does, of course, have some responsibility for keeping the restaurant and its furnishing clean as indicated in chapters "Preparing for Service" (6) and "Snack Bar and Counter Service" (14).

Tables

Tables and sideboards are of special interest to the waiter as his work points. Table tops may be of wood, (plain or, as is more usual in good establishments, covered with baize) or covered with glass or patent plastic materials.

Round tables are favoured in higher class establishments

and normally their sizes are: 28 inches to 30 inches diameter
for tables for one customer, 36 inches to 40 inches for two
or three, 44 inches to 48 inches for four or five, and up to
60 inches for tables of six or seven customers. This last type
is usually expandable so that the table can be made oval to
accommodate larger parties of up to 14 or 15 guests.

In better class restaurants, each party of customers has its
own table and two parties are never made to share.

In more popular restaurants, square or rectangular tables
of a uniform size are generally chosen. These are not considered so intimate as round tables. Customers may in some
establishments, be requested to share one table which can
accommodate 4 guests. An advantage of square tables is
that two or more can be put together quickly during the
service to accommodate large parties who have not reserved
a table in advance. Table sizes should allow at least 1 foot
nine inches and desirably 2 foot length per cover for simple,
plated service and up to $2\frac{1}{2}$ feet per person for silver service.
Wider spacing is not desirable as it tends to make guests feel
isolated.

Sideboard (or dummy waiter)

For efficient service in the restaurant, each waiter needs his
own sideboard or station service table. This normally consists of an upper shelf on which the waiter effects all his
preparations during service. Because of this usage, a clear
space of good size is necessary. Often an electric or spirit-
heated hot plate may also be accommodated on this top
surface.

Under the sideboard top are drawers or compartments,
open or partially open at the front. Here are arranged all
the spare table silver (cutlery) available. (This arrangement
is further considered in Chapter 6 "Preparing for Service".)

Below the cutlery compartments it is normal to have another shelf for storing plates of the various sizes and usages, consommé and coffee saucers and so on.

Finally on a second lower shelf is space for spare linen, tablecloths, napperons, service cloths, napkins, etc. There is sometimes built in to the back or side of a station sideboard a cupboard with slot or flap for temporary storage of used linen.

Sideboard shelves are usually covered with white cloths made from old tablecloths. Napkins or tablecloths should not be used to cover the service table.

Trays

The use of trays by waiters is mostly confined to breakfast or afternoon tea service when a rectangular type is used. Wine waiters use trays or salvers at all meals for the service of drinks served in glasses (whisky, gin, aperitifs, beer, minerals, etc.) and also for removing dirty glasses from tables. Wine waiters' trays are round, in effect salvers, usually from 12 to 18 inches in diameter, the larger size normally being used for clearing.

Square or rectangular trays are sometimes used for carrying food from kitchen servery to sideboard during meal service and also for clearance of dirties from the restaurant.

Trays used for carrying food and dishes should be covered with a clean napkin. (Loading trays is further considered in Chapter 9.)

Reception Desk

Normally, at the entrance to the restaurant is a high desk used by the Reception Headwaiter. On it lies the book where table reservations are entered and also a telephone.

It is customary to keep in the drawer of this desk the keys for linen cupboard, condiment lockers, etc.

Buffet

Also by the door it is usual to find a long table covered with a large tablecloth draped right down to the ground. This is the cold buffet table. It has been placed there so that incoming guests can see at a glance what cold dishes are available. This buffet is arranged just before lunch service. It must be made as attractive as possible, the most decorative dish being used as a centre-piece with other dishes placed on either side. Overloading must be avoided, as this would spoil the look of the buffet. Often a raised centre is created on the buffet by using specially made shelves or with boxes also covered with a white cloth.

Silverware

TABLE SILVER CONSISTS OF:

Soup spoons: for soup when served in plates

Fish knives and forks: for fish and hors d'oeuvre

Large knives and forks: for entrée and main course. (Meat, poultry, etc.). Forks only for macaroni, gnocchi, etc.

Fork with dessert spoon (or table spoon) for spaghetti

Dessert or sweet spoons and forks: for all sweets served on plates and oeuf sur le plat. Spoon alone for soup served in cups, hot and cold cereals

Small silver fruit knives and forks: for fresh fruit

Small knives for side plates for cheese and for savoury (used with a sweet fork)

Teaspoons: for teas, fruit cocktails, ice cream served as "coupes", grapefruit, oeuf en cocotte, etc.

Sundae spoons: may be provided for ice cream desserts

Coffee spoons: for coffee

Service spoons and forks: for serving all food orders from the serving dish on to the plate

SILVER FOR SERVING FOOD:

Soup tureens, double and large
Individual soup bowls
Sauce boats and trays
Oval flats and covers
Oval or round vegetable dishes and covers
Soufflé cases, double
Oval or round under dish for vegetables
Oval or round entrée dishes
Oval or round under dishes for entrée
Round flats and covers

SILVER FOR SERVING DRINKS:

Salver, for serving, 12 inches diameter (round)
Salver, for clearing, 20 inches diameter (round)
Ice tongs for all iced drinks
Ice buckets and ice bucket stands

STILL ROOM SILVER:

Coffee pots — $\frac{1}{2}$ pint and 1 pint
Hot milk jugs — $\frac{1}{2}$ pint and 1 pint
Tea pots — $\frac{1}{2}$ pint, 1 pint and $1\frac{1}{2}$ pint
Hot water jugs — $\frac{1}{2}$ pint, 1 pint and $1\frac{1}{2}$ pint
Cold milk jugs — $\frac{1}{2}$ pint and 1 pint
Cream jugs — $\frac{1}{12}$, $\frac{1}{4}$ pint and $\frac{1}{2}$ pint
Toast racks — 5 bars, 7 bars and 9 bars
Egg cups

SPECIAL TABLE SILVER:

Sugar tongs for loaf sugar   Set of cruets
Asparagus tongs   French mustard spoons

Grape scissors

Nut crackers

Pastry forks

Oyster forks

Finger bowls (can be glass)

Sugar bowls

Lobster picks

Lobster crackers

Ice cream coupes

Pepper mills (can be of wood)

Sauce ladles — $\frac{1}{8}$ pint

Soup ladles

Gateau slice

Pickles forks

Oil and vinegar sets

MISCELLANEOUS EQUIPMENT:

Warm plate for service table

Methylated spirit or gas lamp for preparation of dishes
    in front of customer

Chafing dish

Silver duck press

Silver hot trolley

Rotary hors d'oeuvre trolleys

"Table top" sweet trolleys

Plates

There are several main types of plates used in the service of
food, normally:

Soup plate. Usually 9 inches and used for all thick soups,
    pot au feu (unless a marmite is used), mussels and
    oysters, Irish stew, Lancashire hot-pot

Entrée plates: normally of $8\frac{1}{2}$ inch size are used for hors-
    d'oeuvre, fish and entrées as subsidiary courses, as a
    soup under plate, as a cover plate and service plate

Meat or fish plate: usually 10 inches for main course
    service

Sweet plate: for sweets and puddings (often the $8\frac{1}{2}$ inches
    plate is used)

Cereal plate: deep $7\frac{1}{2}$ inch plate used for porridge and cereals at breakfast and, at other meals, for milk puddings or compôtes.

Dessert or fruit plate: (often of different design, e.g. Bavarian fruit pattern)

Tea plate: for bread and butter, cakes, etc. (This is usually of a floral pattern for afternoon tea)

Side plate: 7 inch size is used for cheese, bread, rolls

Salad plate: (half-moon)

Cups

There are four kinds of cups for use in the service of beverages:

Soup cup: (two handles), $\frac{1}{2}$ pint
Breakfast cup: Plain pattern, $\frac{1}{2}$ pint
Tea cup: Floral, dainty pattern, $\frac{1}{4}$ pint or $\frac{1}{3}$ pint
Coffee cup: Floral, dainty pattern, $\frac{1}{8}$ or $\frac{1}{6}$ pint

Other Equipment

(Equipment made in a variety of materials, including silver)

Ash trays	Flower vases
Bread boats	Fruit stands
Casseroles: for prepared foods and sauces	Ice coupes
	Tea strainers
Cheese scoops	Wine cradles
Crumb scoops	Wine funnels

Glassware

Glasses are separately listed in Chapter 13 "Wines, Drinks and Tobacco".

Service-Room or Pantry

A clean and orderly service-room is essential to an efficient restaurant.

A service-room or pantry contains shelves or cupboards for stacking glassware, etc., a table (very often of two tiers) to take the dirty plates and silver brought in from the restaurant, a box or boxes for dirty table silver, bins for rubbish, and sinks, with hot and cold water and draining racks, for washing glasses.

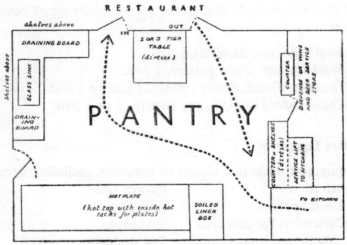

Fig. 1.—Pantry—specimen layout.

If a small service-lift is used, then more shelves should be available alongside it to facilitate the service during peak hours.

In some establishments the glass pantry is a separate unit staffed by those who are used to handling glassware.

A large linen-box (similar to a post-box but with a larger "mouth") should stand in one corner to receive used table napkins, tablecloths, etc. If this box has a flat top it can easily be used for extra service space.

A "hot-plate" (a specially heated table-cupboard with a hot flat top, inside which a supply of hot plates can be kept), forms an essential part of the equipment.

Generally there is also a dispense bar or "wine stores control" adjoining the pantry, so that waiters or waitresses can collect orders for wines, beers, minerals, etc., ordered by the customers.

There should be two doors connecting the service-room with the restaurant: one should be used by waiters going from the service-room to the restaurant, and the other for their return. In well-regulated establishments it is an offence to use the wrong door, for by so doing serious accidents and clashes can happen. The words "In", "Out" will probably be marked on the doors. Fig. I illustrates a well-designed service-room or pantry.

A waiter leaving the restaurant with used materials puts the dirty plates, properly stacked (as explained in Chapter 9), on the table provided, and the dirty silver in the appropriate boxes. (These tables and boxes should be as near the exit door from the restaurant as possible and between the door and the service lift if there is one, in order to save fatigue and consequent breakages). He then goes to the service-table, in the service-room or in the kitchen, to collect the next set of dishes ordered by the customer, (as explained in Chapter 9), takes the plates from the hot plate, and re-enters the restaurant.

4

Meals and Menus I: Cuisine, Courses and Menu Composition

The waiter, particularly in a high class restaurant of the French style, should understand how the kitchen is organised. This helps him to appreciate how dishes are created by co-ordinating the efforts of the various sections (or parties). Moreover, the waiter's efficiency depends to a considerable extent on the efficiency of the kitchen staff. It is, therefore, essential for him to have the fundamental knowledge outlined below.

The staff of a kitchen may consist of:

1. THE CHEF (or Head Chef)—*Chef de Cuisine* (or maître chef). Controls all the sections and their chefs (parties and chefs de parties). Supervises preparation, cooking and service of food from kitchen to all dining rooms. Arranges the menus. Plans the timing for completing food production for the beginning of restaurant service. Checks food for flavour and seasoning by tasting. Supervises the servery (personally or by delegating to his deputy the first sous chef) giving dishes a final inspection before service, with attention to correct garnish and appearance.

2. SAUCE COOK—*Chef saucier*. Makes sauces for various savoury dishes and prepares entrées. He may also act as sous chef (principal assistant to the chef de cuisine).

3. LARDER COOK—*Chef garde manger.* Is in charge of the "cold kitchen" and the preparation of hors d'oeuvre, cold meats, canapés, sandwiches, salads, mayonnaise, dressings, etc. He also prepares cuts of meat, fish, poultry, and game for treatment by other appropriate chefs de partie (though fishmonger, butcher and poulterer may have separate "shops" in big kitchens). The chef garde manger may also act as sous chef.

4. VEGETABLE COOK—*Chef entremettier.* Cooks all vegetables, egg dishes and farinaceous dishes (Italian pastes, etc.) including vegetable garnishes.

5. SOUP COOK—*Chef potager.* Prepares and cooks soups.

6. ROAST COOK—*Chef rôtisseur.* Roasts meat and poultry and prepares savouries. He is also responsible for grilling (though there may be a subordinate grill cook —chef grillardin) and for deep frying of potatoes.

7. FISH COOK—*Chef poissonier.* Prepares and cooks fish dishes and their accompanying sauces.

8. PASTRY COOK—*Chef pâtissier.* In charge of the pâtisserie where sweet dishes and desserts are prepared including pastry, cakes, jellies, and ices.

9. RELIEF COOK—*Chef tournant.* An experienced cook who relieves other chefs de partie when they are away on day off, sickness, holiday, etc.

10. STAFF COOK—*Chef communar.* In charge of staff catering.

11. BREAKFAST COOK. Early duty cook (often of limited training) who prepares breakfast dishes.

12. STOREKEEPER—*l'économe.* In charge of commodity store.
Stillroom staff, responsible for hot beverages, toasts,

etc., are not usually regarded as part of the kitchen brigade but, like the silver and plate wash, usually come under the supervision of the restaurant manager or maître d'hôtel. Stillroom work is outlined in Chapter 12.

The brigade of chefs is, however, supported by kitchen porters, vegetable preparation assistants, pot washer (plongeur) and kitchen clerks. Of the latter, the following comes into contact with waiting staff.

13. ANNOUNCER—*Aboyeur* (literally "barker"). The kitchen clerk who calls out to the kitchen the orders brought to the servery by the waiters. In a large restaurant such as that of a high class hotel, the principal cooks may have one or more assistants, according to the size of the establishment. The more complete brigades were originally organised for à la carte service from a menu of many choices in the French style. In typically British services of set menus (table d'hôte) of modest scope, the same amount of specialisation is not required and cooks can combine duties to reduce the number of sections.

Foods and Cookery

The foregoing outline of the work of the brigade of chefs indicates how complicated is the work of the cuisine and that a chef needs years of training and experience. The waiter is not expected to know about cookery in anything like the same way as a chef. The waiter should, however, have an understanding of these elements that affect his work. For instance, he should certainly know how much time will elapse between ordering a particular dish and its being served, when certain foods are in season, basic modes of cooking, and the meaning of the more common terms, usually French, on the menu. The most essential words are those for the commonest items of food (e.g. the meats, cuts, vegetables, etc.), chief styles of cooking (boiled, grilled, etc.) and the modes of dressing or garnishing.

A basic selection of this information about foods, cooking, times and terms is provided in the lists which follow. Waiters must appreciate, however, that modes of dressing dishes as codified in the repertoires of "classic" cookery number many hundreds.

Chefs in naming dishes have, of course, been influenced by the fact that professional cookery of the western world evolved in France; so that the culinary code is fundamentally a French one. Some kinds of preparations may be simple peasant (à la paysanne) style, others bourgeois (à la bourgeoise) or linked with hunting (chasseur). Many dish styles were named for people (Henri IV, Rossini, Melba, etc.), others for kinds of people à la reine (queen), à la princesse (princess), for places (perhaps where the food flourished, e.g., Argenteuil for asparagus), for battles (Marengo and Creçy) or even after the inventor chefs or their places of work, e.g., Reform (from the Reform Club) or Careme (after the great Regency chef). Experience and study aids the waiter to expand his knowledge of menus, dish designations and food jargon.

Meanwhile, the summaries which follow may be regarded as a basis which a waiter can augment from his experience and his own notes during his years of training and in the restaurant.

Common Modes of Cooking

Styles of cooking usually appear on menus in the form of a past participle describing a noun; for example rôti (meaning roasted) is the past participle of rôtir, to roast. It describes gigot (meaning leg) in the phrase: gigot d'agneau rôti. Gigot is a masculine, singular noun but when rôti has to describe a feminine noun it will change as French adjectives normally do, by the addition to it of "e" for feminine and "s" for plural or both "es" for feminine plural—hence pommes rôties for roasted potatoes.

Waiters must appreciate that there will inevitably and correctly be such changes of spelling of such words on menus; but for simplicity participles below have been rendered in the simple masculine singular.

Braiser—To braise, by oven cooking in enclosed pot. Hence braisé—braised.

Bouillir—To boil by immersion in boiling water, stock or other liquid. Hence bouilli—boiled.

Etuver—To stew by gentle simmering (often in food's own juice or a little added liquor). Hence etuvé—stewed.

Frire—To deep fry by immersion in hot fat or oil. Hence frit—fried.

Griller—To grill or broil, similar to true roasting but for smaller cuts, i.e., cooking on gridiron over clear fire (often charcoal, gas or electric radiants). Hence grillé —grilled or broiled.

Pocher—To poach by gentle cooking in boiling liquid. Hence poché—poached.

Poêler—To pot roast in covered pan on bed of roots. Hence poêlé—pot roasted.

Rôtir—To roast, cooking by radiant heat before or over a clear fire. (Nowadays, food is often "roasted" in the dry heat of an oven.) Hence rôti—roasted.

Sauter—To shallow fry (literally to jump or toss) in pan with a smaller quantity of fat or oil. Hence sauté— shallow fried.

en vapeur—To cook in steam. Hence vapeur or en vapeur —steamed.

Other Common Modes of Cooking or Serving

Derivative from the basic styles in the foregoing list are further common modes of cooking expressed by French terms such as:

ail, à l'—with garlic.

Anglaise, à l'—in English style, i.e., plainly roasted, boiled, fried with simple English accompaniments.

Aspic, en—Cold in aspic or jelly.

Broche, à la—on the spit, i.e., roasted.

Brochette, à la—on a skewer, i.e., grilled or broiled.

Casserole, en—braised or stewed within an enclosed fire-proof dish.

Coquille, en—Cooked in shell (usually in a scallop shell).

Croquette—Minced, shaped as large corks and fried.

Croustade, en—in pastry.

Diablé—Devilled, highly seasoned.

Eminos—Minced.

Farci—Stuffed.

Froid—Cold.

Fines-herbes—with finely chopped herbs.

Flambé—Flamed.

Frappé—Chilled.

Fumé—Smoked

Garni—Garnished.

Gelée, en—in jelly.

Glacé—Glazed or iced.

Gratin, au—Breadcrumb topped and glazed.

Hachi—Hashed.

Jus, au—with its natural juice or liquor.

Maigre, au—without meat, Lenten fare.

Meunière—Shallow fried (fish) in butter, lemon garnish.

Naturel, au—in simple or natural style.

Orly, à l'—Fried in batter (Tomato sauce separately).
Purée, en—Mashed or purée-d.
Rafraîchi—Lightly chilled.
Réchauffé—Reheated.
Tasse, en—in cup.
Terrine, en—in earthenware dish (usually a pâté).
Vert-pré—with watercress (usually grills).

Common Terms for Degrees of Cooking

The following apply especially to grilling:

à point—Medium grilled, just done.
bleu—very underdone, i.e., charred outside and raw or
    "blue" inside.
bien cuit—well cooked.
flared—as bleu.
rare—underdone.
saignant—underdone.

Cooking Times for à la Carte Service

The following are the approximate times that elapse between
the giving of an à la carte order by the waiter to the
kitchen and its being ready for service to the customer:

DISH	MINUTES
Clear Soup (Consommé) . . .	10
Thick Soup (Crème)	10
Macaroni, Spaghetti (in butter or tomato sauce)	15
Omelette, Fried Eggs	10
Bacon and Eggs (oeufs au lard) . .	10
Poached or scrambled Eggs (oeufs pochés ou brouillés)	10
Fish, Fried or Grilled . . .	10 - 15

DISH	MINUTES
Fish, Poached	20
Calf's Liver (foie de veau)	15
Châteaubriand	20
Grills: Steaks	
Underdone (rare)	10
Medium	15
Well done	20
Lamb Chop (chop d'agneau)	15
Mutton Chop (chop de mouton)	15 - 20
Pork Cutlet (côtelette de porc)	20
Veal Cutlet (côtelette de veau)	20
Game	25 - 40
Pigeon, roasted or grilled	25
Roast Game Birds (for small birds)	from 12
Roast Game Birds (for larger varieties)	up to 45
Spring Chicken (1 portion (poussin) or two portions (poulet de grain)	20 - 30
Chicken (3 to 4 portions) (poulet)	45 - 60
Chicken en cocotte (poulet en cocotte)	40
Chicken wing fillet (suprême de volaille)	20
Potatoes, fried (pommes frites)	20
Potatoes, mashed (pommes en purée)	10
Potatoes, sautees (pommes sautées)	10
Potatoes, boiled (pommes nature)	10
Tomatoes, grilled (tomates grillées)	10
Soufflé	35

Where infra-red or radar range equipment is installed the above times do not apply.

A customer ordering à la carte often states his requirements well in advance of the meal so that the kitchen has adequate time in which to prepare the dishes.

Foods in Season

The statement that certain foods are "in season" implies that they are served only at that time of the year, e.g., in Britain grouse is first shot on 12th August and the oyster season opens on 1st September. Development of cold storage facilities, however, has considerably lengthened seasons for many foods.

Fish

Oysters (huitres) . . .	September-April
Mussels (moules) . . .	September-April
Mackerel (maquereau) . .	April-October
Salmon, Scotch (saumon d'Ecosse) .	February-August
Salmon (English) . . .	March-September
Salmon Trout (truite saumonée) .	March-September
River Trout (truite) . . .	April-September
Sole (Sole); Cod (cabillaud); Whiting (merlan); Haddock (aigrefin (alt. aiglefin); Herrings (harengs); Turbot (turbot); Halibut (flétan), etc. .	All the year

Poultry

Duck, Chicken, Capons (canard, poulet, chapon)	All the year
Turkey (dinde) . . .	All the year
Gosling (oison) . . .	April-September
Goose (oie) . . .	December

Game

Snipe, Woodcock (bécassine, bécasse)	October-March
Quail (imported), (caille) . .	All the year

Wild Duck (caneton sauvage)   In autumn and winter
Venison (venaison) . . July-February
Pheasant (faisan) . . 1st October-February
Grouse (coq de bruyère) . 12th August-December
Hares (lièvres) . . . August-February
Partridges (perdreaux) . 1st September-February
Plovers (pluviers) . . . October-March

Vegetables (Fresh)

Artichokes (artichauts) . . November-June
Jerusalem artichokes (topinambours) . Autumn to winter
Asparagus, natural (asperges) . May-August
Celery (céleri) . . . September-March
Sprouts (choux de Bruxelles) . . September-March
Seakale (chou de mer) . . . December-May
Marrow (courgette) . . . July-October
Broad Beans (féves) . . . June-August
French Beans (haricots verts) . . June-September
New Peas (petits pois) . . May-July
Truffle, fresh (truffe) . . . Autumn-winter
Chicory (endive) . . . October-March

Fruits

Cherries (cerises) . . . May-July
Green figs (figues vertes) . . In autumn
Strawberries, forced and natural (fraises) In summer
Raspberries (framboises) . . In summer
Gooseberries and Currants (groseilles
   à maquereau and groseilles) . In summer
Tangerines (mandarines) . . November-June
Melon (melon) . . . All the year
Plums (prunes) . . . July-October
Rhubarb, forced and natural (rhubarbe) January-June

Composition of a Meal

Since a well-balanced meal is one that satisfies the customer's appetite, pleases him and yet leaves him without any feeling of over-feeding, the various dishes that constitute the meal should be carefully balanced. Otherwise a series of dishes may be selected which are excellent individually, but collectively may make an indigestible meal.

In chapter 11 (pages 142-144) there are specimen menus for a banquet. This is the longest, most varied and perhaps most carefully prepared of the meals that a restaurant serves. The order of dishes is from those that aim to stimulate appetite (hors d'oeuvre, soups, etc.) via light food (such as fish with an appropriate sauce), followed by a light meat course (the entrée), on to the main dish (roast served with a salad or possibly, with vegetable and potatoes). The next dish is invariably a light "sweet" or ice to change the taste completely, followed by a choice of "dessert", fruit or cheese. Finally, coffee is served.

Chapter 13 explains that the service of wines follows this order of stimulation of appetite; first the lighter wines (usually white) and then the heavier wines until the coffee is served, which, as it will be sipped at leisure, may be accompanied by a liqueur to "settle" the digestion.

A *dinner* (implying an ordinary meal of the day, served usually in the evening) is seldom so elaborate as the banquet. Some of the courses mentioned above may, therefore, be omitted. Similarly *lunch* (the term for a meal served in the middle of the day) is lighter still. It may consist simply of three or, at most four, courses, say hors d'oeuvre, fish, a roast or entrée and a sweet.

The Courses

The number of courses served varies with meals (whether

lunch, dinner or supper), type of restaurant, numbers catered for and price charged. The recognised sequence, outlined above, in which the various dishes are served is, however, followed no matter how long or short the menu may be.

The following summarises the nature of possible courses but it is again stressed that a full dinner is nowadays seldom served. Usually 3 or, at most 4, courses suffice for a luncheon; 4 or 5 for dinner; 2 or 3 for supper; 5 or 6 for a banquet.

HORS D'OEUVRE. This course is composed usually of dishes of a tangy, salty nature, aimed to stimulate appetite. The term hors d'oeuvre usually applies to a variety of side dishes offered as appetisers such as potato salad, anchovies, prawns, olives, Russian salad, Bismark herring, gendarmes, sardines, cold egg dishes, or to single items also served as a preliminary appetiser course before the soup, e.g., dishes like melon, caviar, oysters, smoked salmon, salami, sausage, smoked ham.

SOUP (*potage*): Two soups are usually featured on a table d'hôte dinner—one clear (consommé) and one thick (crème, velouté or purée). Only one is served with each meal. The clear soup is listed first on the menu.

PASTA (Italian and other pastes) AND EGGS: Pasta (such items as spaghetti, gnocchi, nouilles) may be served as a preliminary course at luncheon, either in place of or following the soup course. Egg dishes (en cocotte, sur le plat, brouillés (scrambled), omelettes, etc.) may similarly be featured at this point on a luncheon menu. Egg or pasta dishes are usually taken in place of a fish course if hors d'oeuvre and/or soup have been chosen. They are seldom included on set dinner menus, but may be chosen as an early course from à la carte selections by guests taking less formal evening meals.

FISH: Two kinds of fish are frequently offered on a table d'hôte dinner. One is invariably a poached fish served with a sauce mousseline or hollandaise or similar sauce. Plainly steamed or boiled potatoes are usually offered with this type of fish. For luncheon the fish course can be replaced by a hot egg dish such as an omelet or an "oeuf sur le plat".

ENTRÉE: This is the first of the meat courses. At dinner, usually, it is complete in itself in that is it accompanied by its own appropriate vegetable or other garnish. It may be a dish like sweetbreads, garnished cutlets, vol au vent, liver and so on. (A luncheon entrée may be more substantial and sometimes additional vegetables may be served separately.)

REMOVE OR RELEVÉ: is a larger joint or "pièce de resistance" and may consist of a saddle of lamb, a cushion of veal, braised ham or even venison. Potatoes and one or two vegetables are served with this course.

THE SORBET: This course is intended to be a pause during a long meal. A sorbet helps "settle" dishes already served and stimulates the appetite. It is a water ice, usually flavoured with champagne or other delicate wine or liqueur and is served in a tall, small glass with a teaspoon. Cigarettes, usually Russian, are passed at this stage and ten minutes are allowed before the next course.

THE ROAST (rôt): This course consists of poultry or game, such as chicken, duck, turkey, pheasant, grouse or partridge, served with their sauces and gravy. A dressed salad is served separately on a half-moon plate. Particularly for shorter dinners (i.e., without an entrée) it is nowadays possible that a fine meat roast such as a fillet of beef may be served.

VEGETABLES (legumes): The French customarily serve a

finely dressed vegetable as a separate course, for example asparagus served with sauce hollandaise or beurre fondu. But at lunch time (or even at a simple dinner) some may chose this type of dish, i.e., globe artichoke or asparagus as a preliminary course.

SWEET (*entremet*):   This may consist of a hot sweet such as a soufflé or rum omelet otherwise an ice (such as coupe, biscuit glacé, bombe glacée or meringue glacée).   Petits fours (friandises or mignardises) are passed with this course.

SAVOURY: A savoury course usually consists of a tit-bit on a hot canapé of toast or fried bread.   Alternatively, a savoury course may be a hot soufflé (of, say, cheese or haddock) or a dainty savoury flan or ramequin.

Alternatively the cheese platter (particularly at luncheon) may be presented; with biscuits, butter, celery, watercress as probable accompaniments.

DESSERT: This finale consists of basket of fresh fruit (possibly also dried fruits and nuts).   They are sometimes placed on the table as part of the decorations.

Finally, coffee is served and liqueurs and brandy passed.

Menu Balance

In selecting dishes from the range possible in the foregoing courses and in deciding the number of courses; it must be remembered that a suitable menu is one that conforms to:

(a)   The principles of digestibility
(b)   The customer's individual preferences
(c)   Season of the year and nature of the occasion
(d)   The resources of the kitchen staff and equipment and what it is possible to prepare in the time

(e)   Clear cost and price policy
(f)   Balance of foods not only nutritionally and for diges-
       tion but also in terms of varied but balanced flavour,
       colour, texture and consistency.

Regular menus of the day are normally composed by the
chef (or caterer) in accordance with the management's catering policy. But a menu for a pre-ordered party will usually
be compiled by the restaurant manager in consultation with
the chef. The former should know what customers desire,
and the chef what can be prepared by his staff in the kitchen
on the day in question and within the limits of costs that he
is allowed.

It would be of little use to compile a menu of dishes which
could be prepared only with more kitchen staff than actually
exist or which demand much more knowledge or skill than
is possessed by the chef and his assistants. It is obvious that
there is a big difference between compiling a menu for a busy
restaurant which has to serve to capacity and at a high speed
during the rush hours of the day, and making one for a
leisurely banquet.

The following are important points to be considered at all
times when compiling a menu:

(1)   A menu should not contain two dishes which are composed of the same ingredients, e.g., if an egg dish is on the
menu then eggs should not form any appreciable part of the
hors d'oeuvre. This applies to all other dishes, e.g., if the
soup is Crème Dubarry, which contains cauliflower as its
base, then cauliflower should not be served later as a vegetable. If pie or pastry is served e.g., vol au vent then there
should not be any starchy food, e.g., apple pie, served as
sweet.

(2)   Two white meats or two dark meats should never follow
each other, e.g., pork should not be followed by veal, or

beef by mutton. There are so many different dishes that this duplication of taste and nutriment can easily be avoided.

(3)   A light entrée should be followed by a heavier dish.

(4)   If the menu is long, dishes should be chosen that are not so heavy; for example, if a big banquet is being served, earlier dishes in particular, should be without much bulk. Note the possibility, in the middle of an elaborate banquet (say before the roast is served) of serving a sorbet or water ice to stimulate appetite and to counteract the effect of the dishes that have already been eaten.

(5)   If the menu is short, dishes may be included which have consistency or bulk to ensure that diners will have sufficient.

Remember that there are two main kinds of menu; à la carte and table d'hôte. The former is a list of all the dishes within the resources of the particular restaurant's kitchen and from which the guest may select to compose his own menu. The table d'hôte (literally and originally the "host's" or hotelier's own table) is a meal at a fixed price with limited choice or no choice. The waiter may be asked by his guest for guidance in making choices from both kinds of menus.

Whatever the type of menu the waiter should, therefore, be familiar with all the dishes and their composition and should have memorised them. He should also have an appreciation of the fundamentals of blending courses to help compose an acceptable suggestion. Finally, he will often be required to comprehend and then explain to customers French expressions on a menu. He should, therefore, become familiar with the words for food and methods of cookery listed earlier in this chapter. Additionally, he will find useful the basic menu language explained in the following section.

5

Meals and Menus II:
Further Food and Menu Terms

Many menus in Britain today are in English, and this is
sensible when dishes and their range are of our own tradition. Moreover, even when menus are written in French,
there are many establishments where an English translation
or interpretation also appears. Nevertheless a waiter still
encounters the French menu. The lists which follow are
intended to provide a basis for menu understanding. There
is also a short vocabulary at the chapter's end of other
French words often used in the restaurant by waiters.

Menu Names for Food

In the following list, course by course, section (a) names
foods, commodities or cuts frequently encountered on menus.
Section (b) indicates a few examples of common styles or
garnishes normally linked with that course.

Hors d'oeuvre or Appetiser Course

(a) FOODS

Anchois—Anchovies.
Anguille fumée—Smoked eel.
Artichauts (fonds d'artichauts)—Globe artichokes (arti-
choke bottoms).
Betterave—Beetroot.

Céleri-rave—Celeriac.

Champignons—Mushrooms.

Charcuterie—Cold sausage, smoked ham, etc.

Crevettes grises—Shrimps.

Crevettes roses—Prawns.

Escargots—Snails.

Huitres—Oysters.

Jambon—Ham.

Jambon de Bayonne, de Parme—Bayonne ham and Parma ham are varieties of smoked ham.

Pamplemousse—Grapefruit.

Pâté—Paste, hence pâté de foie gras, goose liver paste or pâte maison, pâté in "the style of the house".

Radis—Radishes.

Saucisson—Cold sausage.

Salami—Italian variety of sausage.

Saumon fumé—Smoked salmon.

Thon—Tunny fish.

Tomates—Tomatoes.

Truite fumée—Smoked trout.

Riz—Rice.

(b) EXAMPLES OF STYLES AND TERMS FOR HORS D'OEUVRE COURSE

à l'huile—with oil.

Barquette—Boatshaped pastry tartlette often filled with savoury item such as fish roe, mousse, etc.

Bouchée—Small puff paste case usually with savoury filling.

Canapé—Small bread slice, toasted or fried, garnished with savoury items served hot or cold (also at savoury course when hot).

Carolines—Small choux paste buns with savoury filling.

Grèque, à la—Greek style (i.e., rice with pimento, raisins).

Strasbourgeoise—Strasbourg style (for pâté de foie gras).

Soups (potages) Course

(a) NAMES FOR SOUP ITEMS

Bisque—Thick soup, normally fish especially shell fish.

Bortsch—Russian (or Polish) broth served with sour cream, beetroot juice, pirogs (little dumplings).

Bouillabaisse—Stew-like fish soup from South of France.

Bouillon—Broth.

Chowder—American potato soup, normally incorporating fish.

Consommé—Clear soup.

Crême—Cream soup.

Croûte—Crust.

Croûton—Sippet of fried bread.

Croûte au pot—Clear soup garnished with croûtes.

Fausse tortue—Mock turtle.

Minestrone—Italian, tomato-flavoured broth, heavily garnished with vegetables, Italian paste. Serve with grated Parmesan cheese as accompaniment.

Petite Marmite—Small earthenware pot which gives its name to the clear, strong, garnished consommé served in it.

Potage—Any thick soup.

Pot-au-feu—Beef and bone broth with vegetable garnish in the French style.

Soupe à l'oignon—Onion soup.

Tortue—Turtle.

Velouté—Alternative designation for cream soup.

Waterzoi—A stew-like fish soup.

(b) STYLES AND FORMS OF SOUPS

Bonne femme, potage—Leek and onion soup.

Brunoise, consommé—Clear soup, garnished with finely diced vegetable.

Célestine, consommé—Clear soup garnished with fine strips of pancake.

Crécy, crème—Cream of carrot soup.

Faubonne, crème—Butter bean soup.

Jackson, crème—Cream of potato soup.

Julienne, consommé—Clear soup, garnished with fine strips of vegetables.

Palestine, crème—Cream of Jerusalem artichoke.

Parmentier, potage—Potato soup.

Princesse, velouté—Cream of chicken soup.

Vichyssoise—Cold cream potato soup, flavoured with chopped chives.

Luncheon Preliminary Courses

Italian Paste and Rice

(a) NAMES OF TYPES

Canneloni—Stuffed type of Italian paste.

Fettucine—Strip-type Italian paste.

Lasagne—a form of Italian noodle.

Gnocchi—a small paste "dumpling" of semolina (Italian) or chou paste (French) or potato paste.

Macaroni—Tubular form of Italian paste.

Nouilles—Noodles.

Spaghetti—Finer tubular form of Italian paste.

Pilaff—Rice, usually cooked in stock with light garnish.

Ravioli—Stuffed form of Italian pasta.

Riz—Rice.

Risotto—Cooked rich dish, usually accompanied by garnish.

Tagliatelli—an Italian pasta.

(b) EXAMPLES OF PASTA, RICE, ETC., STYLES

Bolognaise—With minced meat sauce.

Italienne—Dressed with butter and grated cheese.

Milanaise—With tomato sauce, julienne of ham and tongue.

Napolitaine—With tomato sauce and grated Parmesan cheese.

Parmesan, au—With Parmesan cheese.

Eggs—Oeufs

(a) NAMES OF TYPES OF COOKED EGG

à la coque—Soft boiled in the shell.

Cocotte, en—Cooked in small fireproof dish.

Brouillés—Scrambled.

Dur—Hard boiled.

Mollet—Soft boiled without shell.

Omelette—Omelet.

Sur le plat—Baked and served in same dish.

(b) EXAMPLES OF EGG STYLES

à la reine—en cocotte with cream and diced chicken.

Argenteuil—Soft boiled, shelled with creamed sauce and asparagus tips (Argenteuil denotes asparagus).

Berçy—sur le plat, with grilled chipolata sausages, tomato sauce.

Chasseur—sur le plat, with chicken liver and chasseur sauce (q.v.).

Chimay—Hard boiled, duxelle stuffed, coated with Mornay sauce and glaced.

Florentine—on spinach, coated with Mornay sauce and glazed.

(c) OMELETTE GARNISHES AND STYLES/EXAMPLES

aux fines herbes—with chopped herbs (usually parsley predominates).

aux champignons—Mushrooms.

aux rognons—Kidney.

Clamart—Stuffed with peas à la française.

Espagnole—Spanish omelette (served plate-shaped, flat)
with onion, tomato, pimento. Garnish, half stoned
olive and anchovy strips.

Fish Course

(a) NAMES OF FISH AND THEIR CUTS

See also fish listed under Foods in Season and hors d'oeuvre.

Barbue—Brill.

Blanchaille—Whitebait.

Brandade—Dish of salt cod.

Coquille St. Jacques—Scallop.

Côtelette—Cutlet, alternative term for tronçon (q.v.).

Darne—Finest straight cut through middle (usually of
salmon and similar large fish) with bone.

Filet—Fillet.

Fruits de mer—Literally "sea fruit", usually denotes shell
fish.

Homard—Lobster.

Laitance—Soft herring roe.

Langouste—Crawfish, Spiny lobster.

Limande—Lemon sole.

Merlan—Whiting.

Mignon—Fillet of sole (or similar fish) in triangular fold
as cornet.

Morue—Salt cod.

Moules—Mussels.

Paupiette—Fillet (of sole or similar) flattened, stuffed and
rolled.

Plie—Plaice.

Rouget—Red mullet.

Scampi—Dublin Bay prawns.

Sole de Douvres—Dover sole.

Suprème—alternative term for fillet.

Tronçon—Steak, cut of fish with bone.

(b) EXAMPLES OF FISH STYLES

à l'anglaise—Egg and crumbed and deep fried.

au beurre noir—with black butter.

au beurre noisette—with butter heated to nutty stage.

au bleu—Method of poaching (particularly trout) to give
skin a blue tinge.

Carapace, en—(of lobsters) in the shell.

Colbert (sole)—Sole slit on one side, with fillets then folded
back; crumbed, deep fried and maître d'hôtel butter
placed in slit.

Colère, en—for whiting, head affixed to tail, deep fried.

Coulibiac (de saumon)—Special dish of salmon cooked
in paste.

Bonne femme—in velouté sauce with mushrooms.

Dugléré—with white wine sauce, tomato.

Goujons, en—in strips (for frying or meunière).

Maître d'hôtel—with maître d'hôtel butter (lemon, parsley
butter).

Otero—Served in half, baked potato on shell fish garnish
with Mornay sauce coating.

Newburg—for shell fish (usually lobster pieces) tossed in
butter, flamed in brandy, covered with cream and egg
yolk. Garnish, truffle. Serve with pilaff rice.

Thermidor—for lobster. Served in mustard flavoured,
cheese sauce in the half shell.

Veronique—Velouté sauce, garnished with peeled grapes.

Vin blanc, (sole, etc.)—in white wine sauce.

III. Table Settings

Breakfast (1 person). Fish knife and fork are positioned outside, meat knife and fork inside, spoon for porridge or cereals at top (add a dessert fork if stewed fruit is served). Place small knife on side plate. Lay tea pot, milk jug and hot water jug to the right (note angle of handles).

Luncheon (4 persons). Lay on the outside the cutlery used first: soup spoon, fish knife and fork, meat knife and fork. Dessert spoon with handle to right, that of fork to left; small knife on side plate. Lay-up for fewer numbers is similar but adjust condiments, ashtrays etc. for central or symmetrical position. Flowers have purposely been omitted. *Dinner* lay·up resembles that for Luncheon.

IV. Napkin Folding

Elaborate folding of table napkins has fallen from favour in recent years due to possible objections by customers on hygiene grounds (excessive handling by waiters) and, on the part of management, unnecessary use of restaurant staff's time and labour. Nevertheless there remains a demand for, and consequently a use of, decorative folds for napkins on place settings especially at functions.

The three styles pictured on the top row are especially favoured and these are (from left to right): *Mitre*, widely used for functions—often with dinner roll placed within (although this practice is not universally approved as the roll may not always be observed by guest and may be dropped during unfolding); *Cornet*, extremely popular on the continent this shape is useful for giving "height" and "importance" to a table (especially when table floral decor is a low posy bowl). *Lunch Fold*, an alternative to the cornet requires a well starched napkin to be effective. The remaining two illustrated: *Cocked Hat* (bottom left) and *Fan* (bottom right) are less frequently used today.

Apart from the folds illustrated above, the simple single roll as portrayed in the table settings (Plate III) remains a most effective way of placing and presenting a napkin.

Meat Course

(a) NAMES FOR MEAT, GAME AND POULTRY AND THEIR
    CUTS

(i) BUTCHER'S MEAT

Agneau—Lamb.

    „ , carré d'—Best end of lamb.

    „ , côtelette d'—Cutlet.

    „ , gigot d'—Leg of Lamb.

    „ , noisette d'—Boneless small cut equivalent to
          boned loin chop or cutlet.

    „ , selle d'—Saddle of lamb.

Andouille, andouillette—Sausage of pork chitterling type.

Baron, of beef—Double sirloin.

Baron of mutton (or lamb)—Saddle with legs attached.

Bifteck—Steak.

Bitok—Minced meat, shaped as tournedos.

Blanquette—White stew of white meat.

Boeuf—Beef.

    „ , aloyau de—Sirloin, with bone.

    „ , Côte de—Rib.

    „ , filet de—Fillet of beef.

Boudin—Type of sausage (boudin noir, black pudding).

Carbonnade de boeuf—Type of stewed steak with beer as
    ingredient.

Cassoulet—Braised dish of meats (usually pork, goose or
    sausage) with haricot beans.

Coeur—Heart. Also used to describe dainty cut of fillet
    beef, e.g. coeur de filet.

Côte à l'os—Rib cut beef steak (equivalent to a large
    cutlet).

Carpetbag steak—Large steak (usually double entrecôte)
    split, stuffed with oysters and sewn.

Cervelle—Brain.

Châteaubriand—Double portion, thick fillet steak cut from "head" or thick end of beef fillet.

Entrecôte—Sirloin steak.

Entrecôte minute—Thin, flattened entrecôte steak.

Escalope—Thin collop of meat usually veal or pork.

Filet mignon—Fillet from saddle of lamb or mutton.

Foie—Liver.

Fricassée—White stew of white meat or chicken.

Hanche de venaison (Haunch, of venison)—Half saddle with leg attached.

Jambon—Ham.

Langue—Tongue.

Médaillon—Medallion, name for smaller collops of meat such as veal or pork.

Mouton—Mutton (see agneau for cuts and joints).

Navarin—Brown stew of lamb or mutton.

Porc—Pork.

„ cuisse or cuissot de—Leg of pork.

„ longe de—Loin of pork.

„ pieds de—Pork trotters.

Porterhouse steak—or "T" bone (prime sirloin steak on bone) from the large end of the loin.

Pré salé—Mutton or lamb raised on pasture near sea.

Queue de boeuf—Oxtail.

Ragout—Stew, usually rich and well seasoned.

Ris de veau—Calf's sweetbreads.

Rognons—Kidneys.

Rognonnade de veau—Saddle of veal complete with kidneys.

Saucisse—Sausage.

Rosbif—Roast beef.

Tête de veau—Calf's head.

Tournedos—Small round, fillet steak.

Venaison—Venison.

(ii) POULTRY AND SMALL GAME

(See also poultry and game listed under Foods in Season).

Canard—Duck.

Caneton—Duckling.

Civet de lièvre—Jugged hare.

Cuisse de poulet—Leg of chicken.

Crapaudine—Split whole (spatchcock) chicken, grilled and dressed to resemble a toad.

Dindonneau—Young turkey.

Gibier—Game.

Lapin—Rabbit.

Lapereau—Young hare.

Perdreau, perdrix—Partridge.

Pintade—Guinea fowl.

Poussin—Chick.

Salmis—Stew of game.

Volaille—Fowl.

(b) EXAMPLES OF MAIN COURSE STYLES AND GARNISHES

Alsacienne—with sauerkraut.

Américaine—with grills—bacon, tomato, straw potatoes.

Bouquetière—with mixed, turned (i.e., shaped into small olives) vegetables.

Bourgeoise—(with braises) turned carrots, lardons and button onions.

Clamart—Artichoke bottoms stuffed with putrée of peas, château potatoes (Clamart always denotes peas).

Dubarry—denotes cauliflower. With, say, noisettes of lamb —cauliflower topped with Mornay and sauce Madère.

Holstein—Breadcrumbed veal escalope: fried egg, lemon sliver, anchovy fillets.

Maryland—Segmented fried chicken (egg and crumbed) with banana fritters, sweetcorn pancake, tomato, bacon, croquette potato, horseradish cream.

Niçoise—with French beans, tomato, château potatoes.

Polonaise—for poussin, stuffed and poêlé-d, topped with chopped egg, buttered breadcrumbs.

Printanière—with mixed, spring vegetable garnish.

Provençale—Prepared with a gravy of meat stock, herbs, shallots, mushrooms and, usually, garlic.

Rossini—with tournedos, topping of foie gras collop, truffle slice and Madeira sauce.

Soissonnaise—(for braises) with haricot beans.

King, chicken, à la—Diced chicken in cream sauce.

Moussaka—a Balkan dish of aubergines stuffed with minced lamb.

Vegetables

(a) NAMES OF VEGETABLES (LÉGUMES)

(See also vegetables listed under Foods in Season).

Aubergine—Egg plant.

Boutons de Bruxelles—Tiny Brussels sprouts.

Carottes—Carrots.

Champignons—Mushrooms.

Chou—Cabbage.

Choucroûte—Sauerkraut.

Chou de mer—Sea kale.

Choufleur—Cauliflower.

Courge (courgette)—Vegetable marrow.

Cresson—Watercress.

Epinards—Spinach.

Flageolets—Kidney beans.

Laitue—Lettuce.

Macédoine de légumes—Mixed vegetables.

Navets—Turnips.

Navets de Suède—Swedes.

Oignons—Onions.

Poireaux—Leeks.

Pommes de terre—Potatoes (see below for modes of serving). Usually abbreviated to pommes, e.g., pommes chateau.

Salsifis—Salsify.

(b) STYLES OF PRESENTING POTATOES

There are well over a hundred methods of cooking potatoes. The following are often found on menus:

Allumettes—Match size, deep fried.

Anna—Sliced, pressed and baked in mould.

Au four—Jacket baked. Cut with cross incision before service.

Boulangère—Sliced, with sliced onion, stock moistened and baked.

Château—Turned to olive size, blanched then roasted in butter.

Duchesse—Purée with egg yolk, then "piped" through forcing bag.

en purée—Mashed.

en robe de chambre—Boiled or steamed in jacket.

en robe de champs—Alternative designation (literally in field dress) for en robe de chambre.

Fondantes—Large egg shaped, cooked in butter and stock with upper surface thus glazed.

Frites—Deep fried or "French" fried.

Gaufrettes—Lattice-cut, deep fried.

Lyonnaise—Sautée-d with onions.

Nature—Plain boiled.

Persillées—Steamed or boiled potatoes, tossed in butter with chopped parsley.

Pont-neuf—Thick-cut, deep fried.

Rissolées—Browned in fat.

Soufflées—Rectangular slices deep fried twice in order to "balloon" them.

Vapeur—Turned to "chateau" (q.v.) size and steamed.

(c) SOME STYLES WITH OTHER VEGETABLES

au beurre fondu—With melted butter.

à la moêlle—With poached beef-bone marrow.

Farcis—Stuffed, e.g., tomatoes, artichoke bottoms, etc., (Usually duxelle).

Vichy—Carrots cooked in Vichy water and butter until complete evaporation and natural glazing.

(d) SALADS a selection of "classic" salads (with recommended dressings) is included in Chapter X, page 127.

Sweet and Dessert Course

(a) FRUITS

Abricot—Apricot.

Ananas—Pineapple.

Canteloup—Type of melon.

Citron—Lemon.

Fraises du bois (alt. Fraises des bois)—Wood or wild strawberries.

Pêche—Peach.

Poire—Pear.

Pomme—Apple.

Raisin—Grape.

Reine Claude—Greengage.

Tutti frutti—Italian term for mixed, candied fruits (usually chopped) (often served in or with ice cream).

(b) SWEET AND DESSERT ITEMS

au Kirsch—With Kirsch liqueur.

Baba au rhum—Yeast leavened light sponge soaked in rum

Bande de fruits—Long, narrow type of fruit flan.

Bavarois—Bavarian cream; a cream and egg dessert set with gelatine.

Beignet—Fritter.

Bombe (glacée)—Bomb or shell shaped ice.

Chantilly—Whipped and lightly sweetened fresh cream.

Compôte—Stewed fruit, hence compôte d'abricots (stewed apricots).

Coupe—Silver or glass, stemmed dish for service of composite ice cream dishes.

Crème—Cream.

Crème au chocolat—Chocolate cream.

Crêpe—Pancake.

Eclair—A French choux pastry filled with cream or crème pâtissier.

Gâteau—Cake.

Marrons glacés—Chestnuts boiled in syrup to become glazed.

Meringues (glacées)—Sugar and egg white confection (with ice cream).

Millefeuilles, gâteau—Gâteau of puff paste.

Melba, sauce—Raspberry purée sauce. Hence pêche or pear melba—the fruit served with ice cream, melba sauce and cream.

Nesselrode—Denotes presence of chestnuts.

Poire Hélène—Pear on ice cream with hot chocolate sauce.

Panachées—Mixed, e.g., glaces panachées, ices of mixed colours and flavours.

Pâtisseries—Pastries.

Tarte—Tart.

Savarin—Similar mix to Baba but shaped as hollow ring

Suchard—Denotes the presence of chocolate.

Singapore—Denotes presence of pineapple.

Some Common Sauces

The selection below indicates principal characteristics or ingredients of a number of sauces commonly served with meats, fish, poultry and vegetables. As the waiter continues with his training and experience he will, of course, build further his knowledge not only of sauces but of garnishes and the names by which they are known.

Aioli—Mayonnaise (q.v.) with garlic.

Allemande—Reduced velouté (q.v.) with liaison of egg yolk.

Américaine—Tomato sauce blended with lobster butter.

Anchois—Cream sauce, anchovy flavoured.

Aurore—Velouté or Bechamel (q.v.) tinted and flavoured with tomato.

Béarnaise—Hollandaise (q.v.) with chopped tarragon.

Béarnaise brune—as above tinted with meat glaze.

Béchamel—a thick white sauce of milk, flour and butter.

Bercy—Thick brown stock, white wine, chopped shallots and fines herbes.

Bordelaise—Red wine, half glaze, marrow, chopped shallots. Served mostly with red meat.

Bigarrade—Demi-glace (q.v.) with julienne of orange zest, orange juice.

Champignons—White or brown sauce with mushrooms.

Charcutière—Robert (q.v.) with sliced gherkin garnish.

Chasseur—White wine sauce reduced with concassé (chopped and de-pipped) tomatoes and sliced mushrooms.

Choron—Tomato flavoured hollandaise (q.v.).

Demi-glace—Half glaze, i.e., thickened brown stock (Espagnole) reduced.

Diable—Reduction of wine vinegar, wine, chopped shallots with demi-glace (q.v.) well seasoned with cayenne.

Duxelle—A thick sauce (virtually a stuffing) of chopped mushrooms and shallots moistened with wine and demi-glace.

Financière—Madeira sauce (sauce Madère, q.v.) with chicken essence, mushrooms (and, sometimes, truffles).

Grand veneur—Poivrade (q.v.) and Espagnole blended with game blood and essence.

Gribiche—Thin mayonnaise with fines herbes.

Hollandaise—Emulsion of eggs, butter, lemon—warm.

Lyonnaise—Cooked, sliced onions in cream sauce (usually) or brown sauce.

Madère—Demi-glace flavoured with Madeira wine.

Maître d'hôtel—(a) "hard" sauce of butter with lemon juice and chopped parsley. (b) Velouté (q.v.) richened with maître d'hôtel butter.

Marchand de vins—Red wine brown sauce with chopped shallots.

Marinière—White wine fish sauce with fines herbes.

Matelote—as Bordelaise with fish glaze and anchovy flavour in place of meat glaze.

Mayonnaise—Emulsion of eggs, oil, vinegar and mustard —cold.

Mornay—Béchamel (q.v.) with grated cheese.

Mousseline—Hollandaise (q.v.) with whipped cream.

Newburg—Butter, cream, yolk of eggs, sherry.

Périgueux—Madère (q.v.) with truffles.

Piquante—Tomaté-d half glaze, with vinegar reduction and gherkin garnish.

Poivrade—as piquante (q.v.) but without gherkin.

Portugaise—Tomato with onion, garlic flavour.

Poulette—Velouté (q.v.) with egg yolk liaison, mushroom essence and lemon juice finish.

Raifort—Cream sauce with horseradish.

Ravigote—Egg yolks, oil, vinegar and chopped herbs.

Reform—Madère (q.v.) with julienne of egg white, cooked tongue and truffle.

Robert—Demi-glace (q.v.) with white wine, sliced onion flavour.

Soubise—Thick white sauce of onion and cream.

Tartare—Mayonnaise with chopped gherkins, capers, fines herbes—Cold.

Verte—Mayonnaise with fines herbes and green colouring.

Further Common Menu Terms

To complete the waiter's ability to interpret a French menu or understand restaurant jargon he should also be familiar with other words in common menu or restaurant usage; such as:

à la—after the style, or fashion of, e.g., à la française, French style; à la russe, Russian style; also with (or dressed in) e.g., à la crème, with or in cream.

à la carte—on the menu (literally card): implies many dishes at different prices for the guest's choice. Normally cooked to order (as distinct from table d'hôte, q.v.)

au—masculine form of à la (q.v.).

Biscotte—Rusk.

Café—Coffee.

Café au lait—Coffee with milk.

Café double—Double strength coffee for lunch and dinner.

Café noir—Coffee without cream or milk, i.e., black coffee.

Carte du jour—Menu of the day.

Chauffe-plats—Sideboard hot plates.

Couvert—Cover or place setting.

Déjeuner—Lunch.

Demi-tasse—Literally, half cup, small coffee cup.

Diner—Dinner.

Entrée—a composed, garnished dish served before the roast or main meat course (or, at luncheon, served as main course).

Entremet—Sweet course (formerly entremet sucré; as an entremet de legume, separate vegetable course was equally frequently served).

Fromage—Cheese.

Guéridon.—Side-table (for service); nowadays may be a wheeled table or cart.

Mise en place—Literally "put in place" to waiters implies pre-preparation of sideboards, table, restaurant, etc.

Petit déjeuner—Breakfast.

Plat du jour—Special dish of the day.

Réchaud—"Lamp" or small spirit stove for restaurant re-heating or cooking.

Souper—Supper.

Table d'hôte—a set meal, usually of several courses, at a fixed, inclusive price.

Timbale—a round deep dish of straight sides.

Vol au vent—Puff pastry case usually filled with diced chicken, fish, etc., dressed in sauce.

Voiture—Carriage or trolley; for example for hors d'oeuvre or pastries.

Wagon—Alternative name for voiture.

6

Preparing the Restaurant

Apart from the service at table, the waiter has certain other duties to do each day such as preparation of the restaurant, looking after the cleanliness of the furniture and equipment, including ancillary sections such as pantry and locker room. This is often referred to as doing the menage—literally, the housework. In restaurants, as in cuisines, equipment or foods pre-prepared in readiness for service are described as mise en place (put in place). Hence, preparing is itself called in restaurant jargon "doing the mise en place". What has been so prepared is described also as mise en place or as being "en place".

Restaurant Mise en Place Routine

Evening

In restaurants where breakfast is not served or where a special breakfast room separate from the restaurant is available, restaurant tables are completely cleared the previous night. Salt cellars, peppers and other condiments are placed on a table near the service doors, mustard dishes are emptied (contents possibly kept in a jug) and washed. Flowers are removed to the flower room usually within the housekeeper's department. Clean table cloths are all placed on top of one another on one table. All the chairs are placed on tables—seats resting on the table.

Morning

The first duty of waiting staff on arrival in the morning is to open all the windows so as to air the room thoroughly, clearing cigar and other smells. Then each member of staff attends to his particular duty as detailed by the headwaiter. These consist of sweeping the carpet or floor (if this has not been done by the housekeeper's staff) dusting furniture, polishing mirrors and glass shelves, silver and glass show pieces, etc., cleaning and re-filling salts and peppers, wiping necks and corks of sauce bottles, making up fresh mustard and re-filling the dishes, cleaning certain articles of silver (in some hotels all silver is cleaned by dining room staff), changing linen, restocking sideboards, and dummy waiters, preparing the cold buffet table, sharpening knives (this should never be done during the service), and finally setting the tables for lunch.

When all the preparations are over (usually about an hour before the next service begins), all the windows are closed and the room allowed to reach comfortable warmth. The temperature of a dining room is around 65°F. (possibly higher where American guests predominate).

Waiters then go to their dressing room to wash and tidy and clean their uniform. They return to the dining room half an hour before the service in order to put finishing touches to their stations, to attend to trolleys for sweet and plat du jour and to place the cold dishes on the buffet. Lunch is usually served between 12 o'clock and 2.30 p.m., in some cases even later.

Organising Mise en Place

A head waiter or waitress of an establishment is usually responsible for the proper organisation of mise en place and menage duties. It is the rule to assign one or more waiters to each of such duties for a period (say a week at a time) on rota, so that one may be detailed to look after the cruets, another the glass, another the table linen and so on. This, of course, is subject to "house" custom.

In some restaurants, the station waiter is held responsible for all such duties concerning the tables that make up his station (or section).

A relief waiter is available to take charge of each section in turn whilst the waiter responsible for it has his "day off".

It is the waiter's responsibility to ensure that all equipment used on his tables is spotless. He should not blame anyone else for dirty silverware, plates or glasses. He can easily rectify possible dullness, but if anything is not washed properly he should return it for rewashing. The following paragraphs show how a waiter can make certain his "mise en place" is always in perfect trim.

Restaurant Cleaning

Scrubbing floors and cleaning of windows and walls are not part of the waiter's normal duties; this work is left to special cleaners. But he will ordinarily sweep, or vacuum the floor. If it is uncovered, (e.g., parquet) the use of a good hair broom and careful sweeping with the minimum of dust raising is all that is necessary. He should use an electric polisher occasionally as directed.

In order to prepare a restaurant for sweeping, any cloths, silver, etc., remaining on the tables should first be removed to the pantry, and the chairs placed on top of the tables. If labour and time permit, the tables should be moved to one end of the room, the chairs placed on top and the clear half of the room swept: the chairs and tables should then be moved to the clean half of the room, to allow for the other half to be swept.

Rooms should be swept from the windows towards the service doors. When sweeping, the waiter should push the broom and not sweep the dust towards himself. Dust will eventually pile up near the service doors and should be swept into a dust-pan.

When the work is finished, the tables and chairs should be placed in their proper positions, and then be thoroughly dusted.

Most establishments use a vacuum cleaner for the carpets. When about to use this appliance it is advisable to remove all match ends, pins, etc., from the carpet, otherwise the mechanism of the cleaner is likely to be damaged.

Walls and curtains should be dusted before the vacuum cleaner is used in order that any dust may descend to the carpet and be collected. When a carpet is to be swept with a heavy broom, the dusting should be done afterwards, for brooms throw up a lot of dust which collects on walls and curtains.

TABLES should be cleaned. If they are glass-topped, a damp cloth should first be used, followed by a good rub with a dry polishing cloth. Sometimes, when tables are stained, vinegar and water or ammonia and water may be necessary, followed by a rub with a dry cloth. Wooden-topped tables require warm water, followed by a wax polish. Bakelite and similar stain-proof surfaces usually need a damp cloth only.

CHAIRS. Should be properly dusted, not only the seat but under the struts so that no crumbs or dust are left there. Polished chairs should be wiped over with vinegar and water occasionally.

SIDE-TABLES (On which the table silver, linen, etc., are

placed for use during the service), should be cleaned in the same way as other tables. The method of stocking this type of table is explained in the next chapter.

MIRRORS Should be polished with a dry polishing cloth.

PASTRY AND SANDWICH CASES Need cleaning with vinegar and water and a dry cloth.

FLOWERS. Need fresh water regularly, and should be in clean vases. They will be taken out of the restaurant to the pantry at the end of the day's service. Their arrangement is an important factor in the pleasant layout of the restaurant and demands an artistry that will well repay careful study, so much so that some establishments employ a special person for this duty.

Linen Changing

Linen is changed on the basis of one clean item for one dirty item. Counting the dirty linen must therefore be carefully done. Usually a chef de rang and commis are appointed on a roster basis to be responsible for dining room linen stock and for its change. Linen is changed once, twice or three times daily according to the restaurant's size and quantity of stock.

It is a waiter's duty to collect, classify and count all soiled table napkins, tablecloths and slips daily. Usually he is required to record them in a duplicate linen book. Soiled linen is bundled into "tens", after being scrutinised for tears or burns. He takes them to the linen room where they are checked by the linen maid in the presence of the waiter. The amounts entered in the book being correct, the linen maid issues the same number of clean articles.

It is customary, once all linen has been changed, for the

waiter's linen book to be initialled, and the top copy retained, by the linen room; the duplicate remaining in the book. Any discrepancy must be recorded so that missing linen can be obtained later. Linen changing is an important duty and is allotted to a reliable man.

Pantrymen change linen in the same way. In large establishments waiters change their own waiters' cloths and aprons at the linen room. The linen room maid again gives clean for soiled.

Linen Handling

Table napkins may be folded in one of many ways, some of which are illustrated in Plate IV.

Care must be taken in the handling of clean linen. It is easily creased or soiled through carelessness. Waiters should learn which size cloths belong to which tables. Napkins should only be used for their correct purpose, i.e., for the customer and sometimes for clean service such as on a plate carrying cutlery to and from the table. Used napkins, and other used table linen, should never be re-folded. If napkins are only slightly soiled they may get mixed with the clean ones and given to a customer by mistake.

On no account should napkins be used as drying cloths. It is usual to have various cloths for specific work. Kitchen cloths for drying and polishing wet work; dusters (yellow) for dusting and dry polishing; and glass cloths, which should be of linen, for glassware—cotton cloths are not satisfactory as they leave fluff on the glass.

During service the waiter has a waiter's cloth which should always look clean. When he is not using it, it should be kept neatly folded over the left forearm, NEVER tucked under the arm or stuck in a trouser pocket. This cloth is used mainly to protect the waiter's left hand when placing hot plates and serving dishes (see chapter 9 on Forms and Techniques of Service) in front of the customer.

Where a quantity of linen is held in reserve care should be taken that it is used in rotation. Fresh stocks should be placed under those already in the cupboard.

Condiments

(Salt, pepper, mustard, oil, vinegar, proprietory sauces, sugar, preserves).

Cruets, bowls, bottles or other containers or holders of condiments and table commodities should be kept scrupulously clean.

Salt, and pepper containers should be refilled and wiped daily and emptied and washed weekly. (Complete emptying and change should be made, however, whenever the contents become lumpy or damp). For weekly cleaning of silver or plated containers, dry clean the empty cruets with plate powder taking care to brush the screw joint well; refill and replace top. Wipe glass cruets daily and once weekly wash with vinegar solution and small lead shot, well rinse and drain, then place them sideways in or on a hotplate to evaporate all moisture before filling. Check carefully the metal caps of glass salt cellars for signs of verdigris.

Refill and wipe sugar bowls daily and empty and wash weekly. Empty, wash and then replenish English mustard for each meal service. Between meal periods, other containers, e.g., proprietory brand bottles and French mustard pots should also be wiped. Necks and mouths of chutney jars, bottled sauces and similar items should also be cleaned in this way. After day's service remove any plated containers of preserves and sauces and their service spoons for cleaning.

Silverware

This is usually in silverplate known in the trade as A.I. or Hotel Plate. The plating is very thin but durable, and with normal care lasts many years. Nothing should be cut on a silver dish as the slightest cut will injure the silver. Silverplate is easily kept in good, bright condition. The large silver dishes, covers, etc., are attended to by the plate room, but the cutlery and other special silver is often the responsibility of the waiting staff.

CLEANING AND POLISHING SILVER AND CUTLERY. Many brands of silver cleaners are available which tend to be used in private houses rather than by caterers. Cost is, of course, a relevant factor when selecting a method from the different ones available. The following are commonly used:

The Burnishing Machine is mostly suitable for cutlery and small articles of silver. It consists of a revolving drum half filled with ball bearings. The drum is lined with rubber so that the silver is not damaged during cleaning. A special powder consisting mainly of refined soda is used as the cleansing agent with hot water.

The Polivit plate. For large pieces of silver, such as flats, vegetable dishes and entrée dishes.

The polivit plate consists mainly of aluminium. It must be completely submerged in boiling water containing a strong solution of ordinary washing soda. The combined action of aluminium and soda removes stains from the silver in a few seconds. Any silver treated in this way must be well washed afterwards.

The Plate Powder. This is the best method for keeping a hard, bright shine on silverplate, but is apt to take too long for cutlery. It is however, used for very large silver-

ware or articles that cannot be cleaned by either of the
first two methods. Typical items cleaned by powder are
the silver parts of trolleys, methylated spirit lamps, cruets,
bread boats (or silver baskets).

Articles must be free from grease. They are rubbed
briskly with a little moist plate powder (basically jeweller's
rouge and whitening) and, when dry, brushed evenly and
firmly with a silver brush to remove all plate powder,
especially from any engravings, embossments, filigree, etc.
Finally the silver is given a hard polish with a soft cloth—
preferably a chamois leather. It should then be inspected
to make certain that the brush has done its work. If
greasy black marks arrive during brushing, it shows either
that the article was greasy (this can be removed with a
warm moist cloth and the article is then re-brushed), or
that the brush is dirty.

Care of Cutlery

The dirty cutlery from the tables is washed by the plate-room
staff, but not always satisfactorily for immediate re-use. It
is often better if the silver is re-dipped in very hot water and
given a brisk polish whilst still hot and moist. This not only
gives a good hard shine, but also sterilizes the articles. At
times the cutlery becomes tarnished through contact with
eggs, sharp sauces, curries or from non-usage. This can
quickly be removed during the preparation period by
immersing the tarnished articles, which must be free from
grease, in a tank of boiling water with soda and aluminium
plate. A strongish solution will remove the tarnish in 15 to
20 seconds. The silver must then be thoroughly washed and
polished whilst still hot and moist.

Knives should never be mixed with the other cutlery.
They should either be placed in the solution (e.g., Polivit)

separately, or the handles can be polished by the plate-powder method.

Glassware

Glasses and glassware need washing in warm water (not too hot) and rinsing in clean hot water, then drying with a linen cloth. A cotton cloth is not satisfactory as it leaves fluff on the glass, and does not absorb enough water to polish properly. Most pantries have a teak or soft metal sink for glass. Wood is softer than metal and helps to prevent breakages, but the softer type of metal sink is now coming into use.

Water jugs take a "water-line" of chalk or other hard substances in water. This is removed in the normal way. If, however, the water jug has a "neck" and will not allow the hand to enter easily, the method of cleaning is to use potato peelings, finely cut, swilled round the jug with water. Sometimes sand is used for this purpose, but it has a tendency to scratch glass and should, therefore, be avoided.

(*Care in handling Glassware—see Chapter 13 Wines, Drinks and Tobacco*).

Chinaware

The waiter should make certain that his china is spotless. Sometimes it is not dried thoroughly after washing and it becomes dull, spotted, or streaky from a residue of washing powder. This is easily rectified by wiping the china with a warm moist cloth and polishing. A dry cloth only, will seldom remove the marks. If the china still has particles of food on it, it should go back for re-washing. Likewise cups should be carefully inspected to ensure that there is no lipstick left on. Cracked or chipped chinaware should not be used.

Trays

Metal trays are cleaned with metal polish. Silver salvers are best cleaned with plate powder. Stainless alloy trays only require a good wash and polish. Wooden trays need cleaning with a damp cloth and polishing with a dry cloth. Bakelite trays, if stained, should be cleaned with metal polish. Great care must be taken that aluminium alloy trays are never cleaned in the soda tank or they will blacken and be ruined.

Ice

Where the staff does not include a special wine waiter or lounge waiter, the duty falls to another waiter to bring ice up from the cold room and break it for use in ice pails, for iced water and cocktails. Always rinse or "wash" ice that is to be used in drinks.

The Pantry

Including shelves, should be cleaned and the articles kept there (e.g., cruets and condiments) put in order for quick service.

The floor and shelves should be washed daily, the hotplate cleaned with emery paper (if made of steel) or washed (if made of "Staybrite" or aluminium), and the sinks cleaned. Walls, if tiled, should be washed weekly. Larger establishments often employ a pantryman (or woman) for this purpose, who, during the rush hours, when the waiters will be very busy, can help to keep the pantry clear of dirty dishes and silver and thereby assist the service.

Other Minor Duties

Packed lunches may be required for picnics, and hot drinks prepared in advance. Cold pies and cakes may be marked with a knife ready for quick cutting (the knife should always be dipped in hot water to prevent sticking). For very quick service (as in canteens, snack bars, etc.) the portions of the pies may be cut and placed on plates.

7

Preparing for Service

When the restaurant is clean and generally "en place", the waiter must then turn more particularly to his own station to prepare for service. Although some of the following instructions apply to more elaborate services, many are appropriate to good waiting anywhere.

The Sideboard (or Service Station Side Table)

Before the customers are due to arrive, the sideboard should be "en place"; that is, everything arranged "in place"—all the equipment that may be required during service. This equipment should all be laid out according to a recognised plan or sequence. All sideboards should be stocked and arranged in the same, uniform fashion so that there is no confusion when waiters change stations or are relieved on days off.

Items commonly required for luncheon and dinner service on the sideboard include:

Ash trays.
Bread baskets.
*Bottle openers.
Butter dishes.
Condiments: Worcestershire Sauce, Tobasco Sauce, Tomato Ketchup and other proprietory sauces, pickles, Horseradish sauce, chutney, etc.

*Corkscrew.

Cruet: Salt, pepper, oil, vinegar, mustard (French and English).

Cutlery: Soup, dessert, sundae and tea spoons, fish knives and forks, table knife and fork, side knives, coffee spoons and special items as required, e.g., oyster forks, lobster picks.

Doyleys.

Fingerbowls.

Glassware: Water jugs.

Linen: Napkins (Serviettes), Napperons, Tablecloth.

*Matches.

Order (check) pad.

*Pencil.

*Service Cloths.

Service Equipment: Tablespoons, fork.

Trays.

*Items asterisked are commonly carried by the waiter.

Waiters must make sure before service that their sideboard has all that will be required during service. Have ready a good supply of silver (particularly a sufficiency of service spoons and forks), cold joint plates, fish plates, side plates, coffee saucers. The waiter must also see that hotplates are switched on about fifteen minutes before service is due to begin, that sugar bowls are filled and a supply of finger bowls ready for use (half slices of lemon ready for the edge of the bowl).

Linen

Linen having been obtained from the linen room in the manner described earlier in the previous chapter, the waiter should check the number and sizes of all the pieces given him and ensure that they are all in serviceable condition.

The linen should then be sorted according to sizes and neatly stacked on the side-table.

Silver

Silver should be obtained from the plate room (silver pantry), care being exercised that every piece is clean. These should be sorted into knives, forks, spoons, etc., and placed in the respective compartments or the drawers of the sidetable, the handles being kept towards the outer part of the drawer, the prongs of forks and spoons facing sideways.

The order in which cutlery is placed varies according to the number of sideboard compartments available, but it should always conform to a pattern. The items normally placed at the left of a cover when setting a table should similarly be placed to the left in the sideboard. Cutlery placed at the right of a cover should similarly be placed to the right in the sideboard. This sequence should be observed in the same way in all the sideboards in the room.

Placing of more than one item in one compartment is best avoided; but if a limited number of compartments make this necessary then a logical pairing must be observed; for example, pair service spoons with service forks and fish knives with fish forks. It is also advisable not to pair items that are stocked in large numbers such as meat knives or forks.

Other Items

Other items such as ice bowls, rolls of bread, butter, water, doyleys, the supply of which will depend on the kind of establishment, should also be obtained from the appropriate room and placed in readiness on the sidetable.

Note: It is preferable that ice be placed in the water to keep it fresh and cool.

Preparing Tables

As noted below, table laying is usually a group exercise for a brigade of waiters. Each man will take an allotted task throughout the room. However, the procedures involved in laying the cloth and setting the covers may now be outlined.

Laying the Cloth

Catering establishments fall into two main clasess; those which use dining tables covered with a cloth and the others using tables, generally polished, on which the plates are placed with or without an under-mat.

The waiter first obtains the cloths, or mats (usually from the linen room). If mats are to be used they should be placed on the table exactly where the plate, bowl, glass, etc., are later to be set.

Before laying the cloth make sure that the table is in its proper place, in line with other tables, that it is correctly angled and that it is steady so that you do not have to handle it once the cloth is on. A small round of cork is useful for steadying the short leg of a table. When laying the cloth, care must be taken to avoid creasing it as this greatly spoils the general appearance of a table.

When tables are to be covered with a cloth they should be of the type fitted with baize or felt. This is necessary (a) to deaden noise of plates, cutlery and glass placed on them and (b) to keep the cloth in position, to hang evenly without slipping and (c) to cushion the guests wrists from sharp edges of the table.

The tablecloth should be the right side up; this side is always more highly laundered and the hem is always on the under-side of the cloth. The folds should be centred on the table with the points at the corners so that the cloth hangs evenly over the table legs.

Tablecloths are normally screen folded (W) with the face (polished) side outside. This facilitates putting on the cloth. Handle the cloth as little as possible. The aim in laying is to cover the four table legs with the cloth's four corners hanging about 3 or 4 inches from the floor.

To place the cloth on the table, stand centrally *between* two legs, open out the cloth to its length across the table with the two double folds facing away. On the waiter's side are the two woven edges with a double fold inside. The top flap is taken between thumbs and first fingers with the thumbs uppermost and the central folds between the first and second fingers. Keeping the arms outspread the width of the table, lift the cloth and place the bottom flap (which is lying loose) over the far edge of the table. Let the rest of the cloth lie on the table, release hold on centre folds and gently draw the top flap across the table until the whole cloth is opened out. Inspect to see that the drop is even all round and that the table legs are covered. The chairs should then be placed in their correct positions.

Laying the Covers

Having covered all the tables with cloths, the general table mise en place begins.

Tables are laid according to the requirements of the establishment. In à la carte service a minimum is usually put on the table beforehand and the waiter places the necessary cutlery in position after he knows the customer's requirements. He does not, as a rule, lay them all in advance but only as required for each course and at the time of service. In "table d'hôte" service the table is laid in advance to cover all the principal courses, e.g., soup, fish, meat, sweet.

The tables should be laid neatly and geometrically. Remember it is the first thing a customer sees when sitting down. First impressions can make or mar his opinions as to the service he can expect. A tidy table usually means a conscientious waiter; an untidy table, an untidy and careless waiter.

First, "show plates" (entrée plates) are placed at each cover about half an inch from the edge of the table and central to the chairs. Plates must be checked and polished at the sideboards; cracked plates must never be put on the table. If the plates are badged, always place them so that the badge is uppermost facing the guest (at 12 o'clock position) when he is seated.

Then the silver is laid. Clean polished cutlery should be carried in a clean service cloth in one hand (never in bare hands). Handling only at the base, place cutlery at the correct positions round the table (see Plate III).

If a "show plate" is not used, the distance between the inside knife and fork should be a good 9 inches and the sweet or dessert silver (spoon and fork) should also be 9 inches from the table's edge, i.e., a plate space should be about nine inches square. Table ware should not be spread out. The cutlery should be grouped closely. Note the position of the second fork in the photograph.

These tasks of laying the covers are normally done *en masse* during the "closed period". A waiter will thus usually deal with only two items throughout the room.

Two kinds of covers are set, according to the category of establishment; either the popular restaurant offering table d'hôte service or the more costly one giving a là carte service.

As a table d'hôte setting is intended to cover all the principal courses, e.g., soup, fish, meat and sweet, place all the necessary cutlery on the table. Begin with the joint knife on the right of the entrée or "show plate" half an inch from the edge of the table, with the sharp edge of the blade turned towards the plate, then a fish knife and then soup spoon. All these should be near one another without actually touching, and all half an inch from the edge of the table. To the left of the "show plate" a joint fork is placed half an inch from the edge of the table, and then a fish fork. The fish fork is placed up a little, so that the top of the prongs is in line with the tip of the joint knife.

In front of the plate is placed a sweet fork, with the handle towards the left of the cover with a dessert spoon above it in alignment but with handle towards the right. Place a side plate to the left of the cover. Place a side knife on the plate. A water goblet or wine glass, turned upside down, is then positioned just above the tip of the joint knife at the top right hand side. A folded table napkin is placed on the "show plate". Finally, a cruet set (salt and pepper only) and an ash-tray are placed in the centre of the table.

In the morning about half an hour before lunch, the vases of flowers are collected from the Flower Room and placed around the room.

Lay-ups are basically the same everywhere, but there are subtle differences in various restaurants, so the waiter attunes himself to the method employed.

As à la carte service requires only that the minimum of silver is placed on the table, just an hors d'oeuvre cover or a fish knife and fork suffices. Other cutlery when put on course by course as the meal progresses is brought to the table by the waiter on a napkin-covered service plate. This napkin-covered plate is used for every article placed or removed from the table. This kind of "à la carte" lay up procedure is much used in fashionable restaurants whether they are dealing with a table d'hôte menu or an à la carte menu or both. Other than the covers, the rest of the à la carte table lay up is the same as for table d'hôte service.

On a round table the covers are always placed between the legs. On a long table a space of 26 to 30 inches should be allowed per cover.

For a pre-arranged party the complete cover is usually set up with the exception of the sweet fork and spoon. The silver on the outside must always be what is required for the next course.

Salt and pepper cruets are always placed on the table; in the case of a long table allow one set for each two covers. Mustards, sauces including those in bottles or jars are not left on the table. They must be passed by the waiter at the appropriate time for the course for which they are required. They are removed immediately after this course has been completed.

Toast melba and butter are placed on the tables before the beginning of the meal but never before the customer has occupied his table, whether reserved or not. If bread or rolls have not been placed on side plates as part of the cover, they should be passed at the beginning, and during the meal as required. Shortly before guests are due to arrive, the waiter turns up glasses left upside down during mise en place and gives them a final polish.

Points to Check

When the table is laid, check that everything on it is scrupulously clean and well arranged. Covers should face one another across the table when four places are set. When only two covers are set, they must be facing towards the centre of the dining room and not facing a wall or a door. Flowers, cruets and other items should be in the correct position to balance the table setting.

Fig. 2.—Changing the Tablecloth.—Note that the soiled tablecloth is drawn towards the waiter who at the same time pulls the clean cloth across the table so that the table top is always covered.

Changing the Cloth During Service

When a soiled tablecloth has to be changed during service, the following method should be adopted. Any articles on the table should be cleared to the sideboard—*never* placed on chairs or on the next table. The cloth should be brushed, if necessary, on to a crumb tray or plate. The clean cloth is then opened out and held between the fingers as described earlier in this chapter. The loose under-flap is then held clear over the far edge of the table and the centre folds also released. Folding the edge of the cloth between thumb and fingers the rest of the cloth will fall lightly on to the chair. The soiled cloth is then gripped at the far outer edges between the back fingers and the palm and both cloths drawn across the table. As the clean cloth reaches its position the soiled

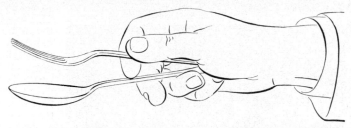

V. Serving

Holding the Serving Spoon and Fork. Note the position of the first finger, which is inserted between the spoon and the fork, giving initial leverage and enabling the food to be firmly held. The spoon is supported by the second finger. Handles of both spoon and fork rest in the centre of the palm, where they can be kept "locked" with ease.

Using the Serving Spoon and Fork. In using the serving spoon and fork to serve a round object such as a potato (as in this picture) the fork is inverted to follow the shape of the food. The serving dish is correctly positioned low down, almost touching and slightly overlapping the guest's plate.

Serving Coffee. The waiter inclines the pot downwards, making a pivot of the part of the base exactly under the spout. The pivot point remains on the tray. Silver jugs are usual for serving milk with coffee but there is a strong case for china milk jugs on grounds of hygiene and easier cleaning. Demerara or coffee sugar may be offered as well as cube sugar. Sugar tongs or a tea spoon should be placed by the side of the sugar basin.

VI. Clearing Plates

Removing First Plate.
This is transferred to
the waiter's left hand.
Note the position of
thumb, little and third
finger on top; other
two fingers below. The
used fork is placed
prongs upwards and
the knife put at right
angles under the bridge
part of the fork. An
alternative (favoured
on the continent) is to
reverse the fork's
position i.e. with prongs
downwards thus
forming a larger bridge
under which to slide
the knives. Both
methods are acceptable.

Second Plate Stage.
The second plate is
balanced on three
points formed by the
knuckle of the thumb,
tips of little and second
finger and lower part
of forearm (the wrist
itself should not be in
contact with the plate).
Next step is to
transfer knife from
second plate to first
plate alongside the first
knife (in the same
position as in picture
above). Then any
food remains on
second plate are gently
scraped with the fork
onto the first plate.
Carry out this
procedure at a safe
distance from guests
and, certainly, never
over the table.

Glass plates are used in this series of pictures to
reveal the position of hands. Service cloth, normally
draping left forearm, has been omitted similarly for
picture clarity.

Stack of Cleared Plates.
Having cleared as
outlined above, the
waiter now has a neat
stack of plates, which
do not wobble and are
not topheavy. Finally,
whilst returning to the
sideboard, the waiter
will place the first plate
(with the cutlery and
remains of food)
on top of the stack.

cloth will drop from underneath. Inspect the clean cloth for correct drop, etc.

Relaying the Table During Service

The flowers, cruet, etc., are replaced on the table and the table relaid with the cutlery, one couvert at a time, from a cloth-covered salver. During service, cutlery should never be carried in the hand, even in a cloth, but always on a salver or large plate which has been covered with a serviette to deaden any noise. The relay silver should be arranged neatly on the salver with the spoons and forks in line on their sides, and the knives and fish knives tucked underneath at right angles on either side. This facilitates handling, allays noise, possible accident, and looks neater.

8

Receiving Guests and Taking Orders

When a guest enters the restaurant he or she should be received and shown to a suitable seat—usually by the head waiter.

Reception by Head Waiter

In large, first class establishments, there is one or more head waiters exclusively engaged on receiving guests. This reception head waiter takes advance bookings and enters them in the restaurant reservation book. He receives the customers at the door with the traditional greeting: "Good morning, (or afternoon, or evening) Sir (or Madam). How many are there in your party, please?" in a clear and affable tone of voice. This greeting may, of course, be varied to suit the occasion. Having received an answer the head-waiter leads the way to a suitable table and helps the ladies to be seated. He then calls the head wine butler and the section headwaiter or station waiter to attend to the guests.

The head wine butler comes first and after giving the appropriate greeting, will enquire if an aperitif is wanted. When the aperitif order has been given, the section head-waiter approaches the host from the left, unfolds the guest's napkin and offers it to him, places menus in front of him and says in a pleasing and somewhat formal voice: "Good morning (or appropriate time of day); may I have your order, Sir (or Madam), please?"

CHOICE OF TABLE. The actual location of the seating depends on the number of vacant places at the time of entry, the size of the party, and, as far as possible, the wishes of the guests themselves. Some customers may prefer quiet corners, others to be near an orchestra or by a window. It is the duty of the head waiter to ascertain the wishes of guests or to gauge them. At the same time he will use his discretion, so that the guests who are obviously well-mannered and pleasing in appearance may have more conspicuous places than those who might appear to have undesirable qualities or to be not well groomed. This "sizing up" of guests and their wishes is acquired by long experience.

A group of guests who wish to sit together should not be placed at different tables. If the restaurant is busy the waiter should, therefore, know just when suitable places will become vacant or be ready to extend and prepare a table to accommodate a larger number.

Reception at Table

When the guest reaches the table, the waiter should always greet him in a courteous manner, never with a trace of bad humour or over-tiredness. At the waiter's station or table, the guests are again greeted. A gentleman: "Good morning, sir", a lady "Good morning, madam", young people, "Good morning". In a smart restaurant, particularly, guests may be gratified to be recognised and named. Thus if the guest is known, the first greeting may be, for example, "Good morning, Mr. Brown" but thereafter he should be addressed as "Sir".

When the head waiter has shown the guests to the table, he should see that they are properly seated; he may do this himself with, if necessary, the assistance of the station waiter, or he may leave it to the latter while he attends to new arrivals. If there is one guest only the waiter will stand by the chair and move it slightly to make it convenient for him to sit down, taking care to move it firmly but carefully. If there are several in the party the waiter will attend first to the lady guests—unless the gentlemen accompanying them do so.

Ladies should be assisted in removing wraps, which should be placed over the backs of the chairs. If touching the floor, the wrap ends should be lightly tucked under the sides of the chairs. At the end of the meal, when they are ready to leave, the ladies should be assisted again with their wraps and the chairs should be pulled back.

How to Take an Order

The waiter should know what is on the menu and be able to advise accordingly. He will approach the guest from the left, deal with the guest's napkin if necessary, place the menus ensuring they are clean, in front of him and enquire: "May I have your order, sir (madam)?" He should wait patiently, facing the guests, until (after any necessary advice has been asked and given) the order is completed as far as and including the main course.

When the menus (table d'hôte and à la carte) are long and varied it is advisable to allow customers a few minutes before asking for the order. The waiter may, during this time, be offering bread rolls and send his commis, with the appropriate checks, to the still room for the butter and, if used, melba toast. Indeed, in good class establishments, when guests are just received and considering their requirements, it is customary for the waiter to place fresh butter on the table, pass bread rolls and fill water glasses. It is also usual for a waiter to assist by unfolding table napkins, offering or helping to place them for guests. In more modest establishments and where, for example, butter is not included with the cover but only as a charged item then this procedure may be modified.

Whilst taking an order it may be necessary for a waiter to enquire about such dishes as chops, "How do you like them cooked, sir—under, medium or well done?".

When it is apparent that there is a host, take his instructions first, otherwise receive orders as guests are ready. It may be prudent to link first orders with individuals by brief aide memoire notes, e.g., host, blue frock, moustache, etc., or, better still, to give each seat a number. If in any doubt, repeat an order back to the guest to avoid error.

TABLE D'HOTE, À LA CARTE AND PLAT DU JOUR ORDERS. There are two principal methods of ordering meals—à la carte and table d'hôte. When a customer orders à la carte he chooses whatever dishes he may desire from all those on the à la carte menu; the charge for the meal will be the sum total of the prices of individual dishes served to him. In table d'hôte service, however, the customer chooses the dishes from a more restricted list (usually divided into courses) and pays a fixed, inclusive charge for the meal.

Some establishments carry each day on the à la carte menu a dish called "Plat du jour". This is frequently also a main dish of the table d'hôte meal. When a dish is the plat du jour it is on the à la carte menu at a fixed price, often less than the price normally charged for it on other days. Potatoes and vegetables as a garnish are often included in the price of a "plat du jour". This dish is always a "ready dish". It is not a means of getting rid of kitchen "left overs".

A good waiter will be aware not only of the plat du jour or speciality of the day but also of seasonal dishes to recommend. Other factors to note in taking orders and, in effect, helping to "sell" the food and service of the restaurant include:

1. Knowing dishes ready for quick service to guests in a hurry.
2. Items suitable for children.
3. Salad, vegetable and potato suggestions for grills, roasts and main courses for à la carte guests.
4. Suggestions for the dessert course when this stage is reached by à la carte customers.

Attending to the Order

If the waiter is busy and cannot attend to a customer at once, he should inform him that he will attend to him immediately or "in a moment". Customers may become impatient if they cannot "catch the waiter's eye". They may rightly be annoyed if a waiter apparently ignores them or passes them without giving some indication that he is aware that they have not been attended to. This often happens when a busy waiter from a different station is passing an occupied table not on his station. He should stop and acknowledge the call—but say politely, "I will send your station waiter to you, sir". Waiters should remember that they are a team and assist one another whenever possible to keep a constant contact with all clientele. A waiter must also be careful when two tables are occupied at approximately the same time that he takes the order of the first party first. Customers are apt to note with annoyance any failure to observe a "first come, first served" sequence.

The good waiter will always either suggest an aperitif at table or a wine or ensure the early attendance of the wine waiter to take these orders. Co-operation between staff is an essential part of a smoothly running restaurant, but waiters should not "overlap" other stations or they may cause confusion.

If the table is laid for service of both soup and hors d'oeuvre or fish, and the customer has not ordered any of these dishes, the waiter should now remove the corresponding silver. When anything on the table is no longer required it should always be removed, on a plate covered with a serviette.

The Wine Order

By the time the food order has been taken, the wine butler has normally attended to and served the aperitifs. The wine butler then returns to the table and presents the wine list to the host from the left, remaining at hand ready to answer any queries and, if required, advise the customer on the choice of wines to match the food ordered. Chapter 13 on Wines, Drinks and Tobacco deals further with the service of wine.

How to Record an Order

The waiter should write in the corner of the next unused sheet of his order pad the number of the table being served. He then records (using abbreviations) the dishes that are ordered. The writing must be clear for it has to be read by other people.

Many waiters' books are made out in duplicate, the original being given to the kitchen clerk before he will transmit the order to the chefs or parties concerned. The carbon copy is retained as the waiter's own record (i.e., number and kind of meal served). It may even serve additionally as the bill that will be presented to the customer at the end of the meal (refer to Chapter 14 on "Checking, Control and Presenting the Bill" for further details of system.) Sometimes two carbon copies are made out, the original for the kitchen clerk, one for the preparation of the customer's bill and the other for the waiter.

Information normally required on the order includes: the waiter's code number or his station number, table number, number of guests and the date as well as details of dishes, price and type of meal ordered.

The order for sweets, desserts and cheese are taken in a similar manner when guests have completed their main course.

How to Pass the Order to the Kitchen

The waiter will know the order of service of dishes that his customer has ordered. He will, therefore, go (or send his commis) to the appropriate part of the kitchen where he will give in the order (stating it in a clear voice) to the kitchen clerk or whoever is accepting the orders, handing over to him the check he has made out.

The dish will then be given to him. In order not to keep the customers waiting, the first dish on the menu is usually one that is ready for immediate service, e.g., soup or hors d'oeuvre. This dish will be taken and served to the customer immediately, unless the dishes following are likely to require lengthy preparation. In this case, timing may be adjusted.

Meanwhile, the dishes that are to follow are immediately put into preparation. These dishes, such as fish, poultry or meat may require to be fried, roasted or grilled or cut from the joint. The final course is usually a sweet course and will come from the pastry section of the service table or pastry larder. It may already be prepared (e.g., cold dishes which will need only to be apportioned) or (in high-class restaurants) it may be prepared for each customer and take up to, say, 30 minutes from the time the waiter first placed the order.

Co-ordinating Orders

Having served one course, the waiter goes to the kitchen for the next course, which he brings to the side-table in time to take away the customer's used plates and to serve his next course.

He should check other tables at his station before leaving the restaurant for the kitchen or service area to ensure that no other guests are trying to attract his attention.

Where a waiter has several separate customers to attend to at one time he must have a clear memory and service skills to obtain and serve the various dishes promptly and correctly. Since each course of the meal takes time to be eaten a waiter has, in the meantime, about 5 to 10 minutes to serve a course to other guests. As he may have up to sixteen or more customers, it may happen that at any one time during the service, some customers will be at the first course stage, others the second, still others the third or final course. The waiter must co-ordinate his journeys to the kitchen to obtain the next courses that are required for each of these.

Order of Service

In a party of *two*, a lady and gentleman, serve the lady first.

In a party of four, consisting of two ladies and two gentlemen, serve the lady on the right of the host first, then the lady on his left, the gentleman opposite the host and finally the host.

In a party of six, three ladies and three gentlemen, the host and hostess will sit facing each other. The lady on the right of the host is served first, then the lady on the left, then the hostess. Next, the gentleman on the right of the hostess is served, then the one on the left of the hostess and, finally, the host.

In a large party, but with a host rather than a chairman, the guest of honour, who is sitting on the right of the host is served first (in a mixed party this is usually a lady), then the guest on his left, then the host himself. The other waiter on the top table of a large party of this kind starts with the first guest on the right of the guest of honour. (For order of function service see Chapter 11.)

In a smaller party with a host, the lady on the right of the host is served first, then the lady on his left. The waiter then continues round the table to the right regardless of sex, serving the host last.

During the service, if there is any undue delay in obtaining an order, the customer must be informed by the head waiter who will offer a suitable excuse.

9

Forms and Techniques of Service

There are several main forms of restaurant service from simple "plated" meals (i.e., food portioned directly on to customers' plates in the kitchen or servery) to elaborate forms of guéridon (side table) service. The principal types of service may, however, be adapted, simplified or elaborated to conform with the "house style" of a restaurant. Moreover, names given to various forms of service tend to differ from one country to another. However, the chief modes as understood in Europe may be summarised thus:

French Service

The fundamental element of true French service (which, of course, emanates from France) is that it affords guests the opportunity to help themselves to the dishes. Refinements or simplifications depend on the grade of restaurant.

For small parties up to 3 guests, dishes may be placed directly on to the table. The main dish (possibly on a table réchaud, perhaps of the "night light" type) is positioned before the guest expected to be served first. The plates are placed conveniently near the dish. For larger parties, certainly for tables of 4 or more, a guéridon or side table should be used. In this case, the waiter brings plates and dishes to the guéridon, sets the plates at guest's covers and then presents the dishes to guests to help themselves. Often, of course, some preliminary treatment of portioning or carving may be required from the guéridon.

NOTE. It is interesting to note that though this is called French service in France, Switzerland and elsewhere on the continent, some British people think that the custom of guests helping themselves from offered dishes typifies an English form of service because this style survives in private houses in this country when dishes are passed by servants.

English Service

This form of service originates in the English tradition of the "master" or family head carving or portioning and serving all at the table. In restaurant English service, the waiter fulfils this role, i.e., the fundamental element is that he serves and at the same time, in effect, decides the portions as distinct from the guest taking his own. Again, refinements or simplifications depend on the grade of restaurant. Generally, English service is also a "silver" service with the portioning largely effected in the kitchen so that food, particularly when it involves a varied or complicated garnish, may be easily separated and served by the waiter. The waiter brings plates and dishes to the sideboard, places a plate before each guest at his own cover, presents the main dish to the host or guests and then passes round the table serving each customer.

This form of service also can be (and in high grade establishments is) effected from the guéridon. In this case, the waiter places the dishes (a lamp or réchaud is needed—at least for the main dishes) with the required number of plates on the guéridon. He serves by completing one plate at a time which is immediately placed before the guest. Guéridon service is greatly facilitated by the use of an assistant waiter to aid in passing the completed plates.

NOTE. Just as there are some misconceptions about French service (see footnote to that section above), so there are in the case of English service. On the continent (certainly, the French and the Swiss and their hotel schools where techniques are taught) know the foregoing as service à l'anglaise (English service) or service à l'ànglaise avec guéridon (English service with guéridon) as appropriate. Unfortunately, some in America especially and also in Britain (including even restaurateurs) are confused by elements such as silver, guéridon or the numbers of waiters involved. Such misconceptions lead to English service being dubbed "French" service—or at its most refined from the guéridon as "service à la Ritz".

Russian Service

The basic element in Russian service derives from the old Russian style of having large joints, whole fish or birds, often decoratively treated on dishes with elaborate garnish, on the sideboard visible to guests before being served. This was then placed or passed for guests to help themselves as in French service. This enjoyed a vogue in fashionable Europe from the early 19th century but its element of display and garnish became integrated into the two other forms of service perhaps particularly English. It survives today only in the sense that in English or French service from the guéridon, it is still commonplace for whole birds (poultry or game), meat joints (especially carrés and filets) and fish (sole, turbot) to be presented whole or in large pieces for carving from the guéridon. Otherwise Russian service as a distinctive and separate form of service no longer remains.

American Service

Fundamentally, this simplified form of service evolved in

recent years depends on pre-plating and the pre-setting of tables with silver needed throughout the meal. Plated food is brought by waiters from the kitchen by tray which is then placed on a tray stand by the guest's table (an elementary form of guéridon). American service may be slightly elaborated by fine table equipment (double coupes for shellfish cocktail for example) and by ancillary serving procedures such as dispensing by separate waiters of hot rolls and trolley or "cart" service for salads and so on.

Plate Service

This means that the customer is served in the simplest manner with food already placed on the plate. This kind of service is used in canteens, many boarding houses and restaurants, where more personal silver service cannot be given. Service is much faster and calls for far fewer staff.

All these above forms of service, and variants of them, are conditioned by general rules of serving. The preceding notes are intended merely to outline their basic forms.

In high-class restaurants, the brigade of waiters is organised on the basic idea that one waiter (the "chef de rang" or station waiter) is in charge of four, five, six or more tables with assistance from one or more "commis". This is fundamental to the carrying out of any good silver service English or French style—especially English Silver Service from the guéridon; for with commis to bring dishes from the kitchen and to do the "fetching and carrying" the chef de rang waiter can attend to the finer points of actual service to the guest.

In further considering the serving of the meal, let us therefore now concentrate on basic forms and techniques involved in all main types of silver service accepted in Britain as the standard of good waiting practice.

Sides for Service and Clearance

The following notes outline basic waiting procedures used in silver service and, indeed, in all forms of good waiting. An indication is given at relevant points of whether plate placing, service or clearance should be from the right or left. The prime rules of the Continental tradition may, however, be summarised thus:

TRADITIONAL CONTINENTAL PRACTICE

Place clean plates and glasses from the guest's right.

Place coffee cups and saucers (with underplate) from the guest's left.

Serve food from the guest's left.

Serve drinks (including wines, etc., and coffee) from the guest's right.

Clear all used items, i.e., plates, cups and glasses from the right.

The above conforms with conventional styles observed in most establishments in Europe, particularly France and Switzerland, and is the basis of teaching in most Continental hotel schools. (The present editors follow the above precepts in their own training restaurant in Scotland).

ENGLISH ADAPTATION. In Scotland there is, perhaps, wider conformity with continental service custom but in many English restaurants and, indeed, in many English training centres, the European mode is adapted—particularly in regard to clearance.

It is stressed that rules or customs of the house as determined by the restaurateur or maître d'hôtel should be followed. Either right hand or left hand clearance may be regarded as correct and this manual does not take up a rigid nor didactic attitude. Guidance which follows should, therefore, be interpreted and conditioned always by the application of the "house" rule of any particular restaurant as to which side of clearance shall be adopted. What can emphatically be said is that once a decision is taken the observance of it should be total. There should never be a mixture of right or left hand clearance in any one restaurant (except when, as notes below indicate, guests' convenience is involved). This means, for example, that a waiter must not interrupt a conversation in order to do his service or force his way between the wall and the back of the customer's chair.

Drinks are served from the right but further detail regarding wine service is contained in Chapter 13.

Coffee cups, sugar (unless it is on the same salver as the coffee itself) and bread are also placed before or offered to the guest from the left. Coffee, as other beverages, is served from the right.

Serving from Silver

When the waiter brings the food, already portioned on a silver dish, he places on it a spoon and fork for service. He stands on the left, feet together, with the dish on the palm of his left hand, which is protected by his folded waiter's cloth. He then bends (advancing his left foot forward) to bring the dish down to the plate just over the rim; the dish being perfectly level. With his right hand he takes the spoon and fork (using them rather like the claw of a lobster) to serve food on to the plate. To do this properly, avoiding breakage or dropping of food, requires constant practice.

Arrange food appetisingly when placing on the plate. Generally, the fish or meat lower centre with vegetables one side and potatoes the other; separate sauces and/or accompaniments at the top right-hand side (2 o'clock). As near as possible, the arrangement on the plate should reproduce the effect achieved by the chef on the silver dish. The kitchen makes dishes presentable and attractive. Chef's good work can be spoiled by indifferent re-arrangement by a waiter (poor service) resulting in food uninteresting and unappetising to the guest.

Should a fish portion be too big for easy service with the spoon and fork, it may be severed across the middle with the spoon. When serving an omelette cut off the extreme tips with the spoon before serving. (Two fork serving is acceptable for certain omelettes fourrées). If an omelette (or other item) has to be cut into several portions, check exactly how many beforehand, to avoid unequal portioning.

Special points to be remembered during service are:

(a) Use a clean set of service spoon and fork for each dish and do not use them again to serve another table.

(b) Do not use a fork without a spoon (except in rare instances, i.e., in serving smoked salmon, cucumber salad).

(c) Never use two spoons.

(d) Never use the same spoon and fork for both potatoes and green vegetables.

(e) When using the service spoon and fork, take care in lifting food that the portion does not slide off the dish to a customer's plate.

(f) Always present a dish to the host for his approval before serving guests and to show it is the dish he ordered.

In more elaborate guéridon services, entailing filleting of fish (particularly Dover soles), carving birds, and finishing dishes such as pancakes, remember that after presentation, the dish should not leave the customer's sight. Such work is performed on a small service table or trolley with a réchaud (hot-plate) or spirit lamp (for cooking) in front of the customer. Where no guéridons are provided, portioning must be done at the waiter's sideboard.

(g) For sweet course service, if the sweet spoon and fork have been placed across the top of the cover, move them down to right and left of the guest's cover—without stretching the arm in front of him.

Use of Service Cloths

Waiters' cloths must only be used for the purpose for which they were made; that is to polish glasses, cutlery, plates, etc., and not to dust furniture, chairs, wipe service tables or clean shoes—nor to flick crumbs off the table. When not in use, the waiter's cloth must be carried neatly folded on the left forearm and, it must be repeatedly emphasised never tucked under the arm. Service cloths must never be allowed to get too dirty; if a cloth gets stained or soiled during the service it must be discarded at once and a clean one taken from the service table. This applies also to napkins used for crumbing the tables or for covering the service plate.

Putting on Plates (Silver Service)

In addition to method of placing, temperature and cleanliness of plates are vitally important. For hot courses they must be hot; for cold courses cold. But hot plates should not be so hot that they cannot be handled.

The pile of plates should be held on the left hand (not between thumb and fingers) which should be covered with one end of the waiter's cloth. On approaching the right (or left, see final sentence of this paragraph) of the customer, the top plate should be given a gentle wipe with the other end of the cloth, and the plate then picked up with the tips of the thumb and fingers of the right hand. Keeping the plate horizontal, it should be lowered into position. This procedure should be carried on round the table, finishing with the host. Check the cleanliness of plates before they reach the table rather than to wipe them in front of the guest; though to wipe the underside before placing is prudent. Plates are usually placed from the guest's right side in Continental styles of service but in Britain there is a slight bias in favour of placing from the guest's left.

Removing Plates

Used plates may be cleared either from the left or the right-hand side of the customer, according to the rule of the establishment (see above, but the whole room must work in the same way).

The waiter removes the used plates directly all the party is finished (but not before), leaving the host until last. Certain priority should be given in clearing plates, first to keep the table tidy and, secondly, to keep from the customer the impression that he is being forgotten. The correct method of removing plates with cutlery is to pick up the plates with the right hand and transfer them to the left. The first plate is held by the thumb lying along the edge of the plate pointing across the body, and the first two fingers underneath, slightly spread. The third and fourth fingers stand up outside the plate—the tips level with the thumb (see Plate VI).

The used fork should be placed with the curve upwards and the used knife is placed under the curve of the fork and at right angles; this is the technique known as the "first plate".

The second plate is placed on the forearm with the under rim behind the thumb joint and on the two extended fingers.

In this way the plate cannot slip forward and the main weight is supported by the forearm (see Plate VI).

Then the knife and fork are picked up and any remains of food are gently scraped on to the first plate. They are then placed with the other cutlery on the first plate, fork with fork, and knife under the forks, as before. The waiter continues round the table in this manner until it is cleared. He should be able to clear eight places comfortably in this fashion (see Plate VI).

By using this method, the waiter has a neat stack of plates which do not wobble and are not top-heavy. When he goes to the side-table he can take the first plate out of his left hand (using his right hand to do so) and place it on the top of the pile so that the whole pile is completely steady. This method is illustrated in Plates IV, V and VI.

It is important that shifting food from one plate to the other be done, as far as possible, out of guests' vision. The angle of the cutlery on the first plate should be such that should anything fall, it will do so towards the waiter and not the customer.

Any articles of silver dropped on the floor must be picked up immediately and taken to the sideboard. They must not be used at the table. Any food dropped on the floor must never be put back on the dish with the rest of the food; it must be picked up immediately and put on a plate and taken right out of the restaurant. This must be done with regard to cleanliness and delicacy, for example, using a discarded menu as scoop but in such a way as to make clear that the dropped food will be thrown away. This is important as the customer is likely to be watching to see what the waiter is going to do with it.

Clean cups, glasses, etc., must be carried on a salver and lifted by their handles or stems and never by putting the fingers inside them. Dirty glasses must be removed by means of a salver and not by hand.

The handling of dishes, plates and cutlery must be done as silently as possible. Glasses must not be allowed to knock against one another as this makes an unpleasant noise. (Some guests may even have superstitions about this.)

Laying and Using a Tray

The use of trays in hotels is generally confined to the service of meals in bedrooms and private suites, also of afternoon teas (see Fig. 3). For the service of a meal in bed the same lay-up applies as for the laying of a table; in most cases the tray will be placed on the bed, or a trestle, as a table. Service in sitting rooms entails the laying of a table in the same style as one would use in a restaurant.

The waiter should balance a tray on his outspread palm on a level with his shoulder (see Fig. 4) so that his right hand is free to knock on the door, and then to open same on obtaining permission to enter.

When the tray is to be carried, it should be laid in such a way that the heaviest dishes are in the centre, with glasses and lighter articles towards the edges of the tray. It is advisable to place the glasses upside down, as they carry in a more stable manner in this position.

In a restaurant, bottles of wine or mineral waters should not be carried on trays; except in the case of wine bottles in cradles or wine coolers. Lounge waiters, however, often carry split size minerals on their trays.

Two hot courses should not be taken in on the same tray at the same time to the same room for the second course is likely to get cold whilst the first is being eaten.

This use of trays applies to all branches of the catering industry. Many cafeterias, cafés and canteens bring food

Fig. 3.—Lay-up of Tray, showing Full Breakfast.—A tray should be so loaded that the heaviest weight is in the middle, the remaining articles being evenly distributed to give correct balance. Bottles when carried should be laid horizontally on the tray; they should not be stood upright.

Fig. 4.—Carrying a Tray.—Note position of hand, central, with tray resting on poised fingers, not flat on palm of hand nor resting on shoulder. For loading of tray for balance, see "Lay-up of Tray", above.

courses to the guests on trays and place the tray on the table in front of the guest. This conforms with hotel "bedroom" service and the tray should be properly arranged in accordance with the general instructions in this book.

Reminders About Service

If at any time a waiter is about to serve some customers with hot and others with cold dishes, he should serve the cold dishes first.

Crumbs and bread should always be removed from the table before serving the sweet or dessert course. Use a neatly folded table napkin as a brush to bring the crumbs to the edge of the table. From the edge they can then be brought gently on to a medium sized plate.

The waiter should remove the cruet from the table at the end of the meat course—just before the sweet is served.

If a finger bowl is served with a certain type of food, it should be placed on the left of the customer; if it is served at the end of the meal it should be placed in front of him, after the dessert dish has been removed.

A waiter should never lay a chipped glass or plate, and should avoid serving from any such imperfect article. If anything should drop to the floor it should be taken to the side-table for replacement. This applies not only to food, but to any article (serviette, knife, etc.) that may be dropped.

No such articles as teaspoons, menu cards or lumps of sugar should ever be kept in the waiter's pocket. The menu card should be on the table or the side-table, never tucked inside the waiter's shirt front.

When serving food in containers (e.g., grapefruit or ice cream), a doyley and an under-plate should be placed under the container.

When serving a beverage the waiter should keep the handle

of the jug or pot away from the customer but the handle of the cup, etc., from which he will drink should be turned to the customer's right. This means that service of coffee, etc., is always from the right of the customer.

Sugar, cream, etc., should be placed at the right of the customer within easy reach.

Waiters must make sure during service that all dishes are properly and completely served, that is that all sauces and condiments required are passed with the dish and that the customer has the correct cutlery.

Waiters should also train their eyes to notice right away whether anything is missing from the table. Check that the customer can reach required items like salt and pepper, observe whether the butter dish contains butter, remember to pass rolls again during the meal each time the guest has finished the one on his plate or that the plate or dish containing toast melba is never empty. These exemplify rather than exhaust points a waiter watches.

10

Service of Courses, Dishes and
Bill Presenting

During the service of a meal, there are a variety of points to be observed at each course. The following notes are intended to give general guidance but it will be appreciated that no attempt has been made to detail the full intracacies of, for example, guéridon service, carving, salad and dressing making and flambé work. (For these more advanced techniques the reader is referred to *The Restaurateur's Guide to Guéridon and Lamp Cookery* published by Barrie & Rockliff).

In this section are provided, however, fundamental points concerning the service of different courses, salads, other accompaniments and some special dishes.

Usual Accompaniments

Many dishes have separate accompaniments and as they are not always mentioned on the menu, the waiter must know them. He should always have any accompaniments ready for service at the right time. Hot adjuncts come with the dish from the kitchen, but cold sauces are often to be found at the buffet or sideboard. They should be served directly with a dish to which they belong. Except in certain instances (mentioned later), they should be served from the guest's left on to the top right of his plate (not on the rim). When serving from a sauceboat, the boat should be on an under-dish or small plate, carried on the palm of the left hand. In serving, the sauceboat lip should point towards the guest's plate. Service is with the same stance as for a main dish. The spoon, or ladle, should be passed over the lip. Sauces should not be poured from a boat.

Accompaniments are summarised following the notes on the various courses below but see also Chapter 5 on "The Meal and the Menu" for a further list. French words for main items are given after the English to aid menu recognition.

Soup (Potage)

THICK SOUP. When serving soup an underlayer plate must be used. The waiter holds the under plate in his left hand, places the soup plate on it and then serves the soup from the tureen using a silver soup ladle. This is normally done from the sideboard. Should any soup be spilled on the soup plate's edge, it must be wiped with the service cloth before being served to the customer (from his left). When removing soup plates, both plates must be lifted at once.

Alternatively, individual portions of soup may be presented in silver soup bowls. In this case, soup plate and underplate is set before the guest. The waiter, from the left, carefully tilts the silver bowl to transfer the soup, away from the guest, into the bowl. For many soups croûtons, grated cheese, flutes, are then separately passed by the waiter who serves them from a sauceboat using a ladle or spoon.

CLEAR SOUP (*Consommé*). These are usually served in consommé cups, i.e., a cup with two handles. The complete set consists of an entrée plate as under plate, a saucer and a cup. All three are served at the one time. The waiter serves the soup from the tureen into the cup with a silver soup ladle and places the complete set from the left. A dessert spoon is used by the guest for clear soup instead of soup spoon.

Soup service is also often carried out from a guéridon which has been placed near the customers' table. A spirit lamp is sometimes used to keep soup hot while it is being served. Care must be taken not to over-heat certain thick soups as they may "turn" or curdle if boiled.

SOUP ACCOMPANIMENTS:

Croûtons (sippets)—sprinkled over soup.
Croûtes (flutes)—sprinkled over soup.
Fromage rapé (grated cheese)—sprinkled over soup.
Lemon wedge—served on left side of underplate with certain clear soups.
Paillettes (cheese straws)—served on bread plate.

Hors d'Oeuvre

Hors d'oeuvre variés are presented on a trolley, each variety being in a "ravier" or similar dish. A separate service is to be used for each variety. The trolley is wheeled to the customers' table and placed near the person who is to be served. The hors d'oeuvre plate (fish plate) is removed from the right-hand side of the customer with the right hand and placed in the waiter's left hand. The waiter must use his service cloth to hold the plate while he is serving the hors d'oeuvre according to the customer's instruction. When the service is completed, he places the plate before the customer from the left. He then wheels the trolley round to the next person to be served and repeats the routine until all the guests have been served.

On certain occasions, a special tray or dish containing several compartments may be used and carried by the waiter to serve hors d'oeuvre. Again a separate item is placed in each compartment. The waiter serves from the dish directly on to the plate in front of the customer, revolving his dish on his hand until he has offered each variety to the guest.

HORS D'OEUVRE ACCOMPANIMENT. An oil and vinegar cruet must be put on the table when hors d'oeuvre variés are served.

The following "single" items are also served as opening courses:

SMOKED SALMON (*Saumon fumé*). This is usually cut (importantly in very thin slices) in the dining room in front of the guest, and placed directly on the plate. In the case of functions, it is cut in the kitchen and the slices are arranged on a silver flat. It is then served by the waiter with a fork only; rolling the slivers round the prongs and unfolding them on to the guest's plate. The cover required by the customer is a fish knife and fork.

SMOKED SALMON ACCOMPANIMENTS. Pepper mill, cayenne pepper and a bottle of chili vinegar are placed on the table. Half lemons wrapped in muslin cloths are passed round. Buttered brown bread, with the crust cut off, are also passed round.

CAVIAR. This is usually served in the original container buried in a silver timbale filled with crushed ice. It is served with a dessert spoon. The cover required is a fish plate and a side knife (or caviar knife if available).

CAVIAR ACCOMPANIMENTS. Blinis, a type of hot pancake or, alternatively, hot toast (breakfast thickness) and slices of brown bread are passed. Half lemons wrapped in muslin, finely chopped onions and chopped parsley are also offered. In some restaurants, sieved egg white and egg yolk are also offered. A pepper mill and cayenne pepper are placed on the table. Finger bowls must be placed at each corner after caviar has been served.

TERRINE DE PÂTÉ DE FOIE GRAS. The cover for this consists of an entrée plate and a side knife. The pâté is served in its original container (terrine) buried in a bed of crushed ice. A jug of hot water and a sweet spoon are all that is required for serving. Dip the spoon into hot water and scoop a portion (roughly a spoonful) from the terrine with the spoon and put it on the entrée plate. Dip the spoon again into hot water before serving the next guest.

PÂTÉ DE FOIE GRAS ACCOMPANIMENTS: Serve hot brioche and/or hot toast (trimmed of crust and slightly thinner than for breakfast service) with fresh butter separately.

OYSTERS (*huitres*). Served oysters on a round silver flat or a soup plate (if individual portion) covered with broken ice. They are opened in the larder a few minutes before being served. The oyster is placed in the deep half of the shell, care being taken to remove the black ring (beard) around the edge of the shell. A half lemon is served with each portion. The oyster fork is placed across the tip of the joint knife at an angle of forty-five degrees.

OYSTER ACCOMPANIMENTS: Brown bread and butter or thin brown bread and butter sandwiches are passed with the oysters. An oyster cruet consisting of chili vinegar, Tabasco sauce, a pepper mill and cayenne pepper is passed or placed between two guests. Plain or other vinegars should be at hand in case called for by a guest. Lemon is an essential adjunct. Normally a half lemon is served with the individual portion. A finger bowl, half filled with tepid water is placed on a side plate covered with a small napkin. This is served to the guest, i.e., set a little to the left above the cover, as he finishes.

Other Single Hors d'Oeuvres and Accompaniments

PLOVER (OR GULL'S) EGGS (*Oeufs de Pluvier*). Cut brown bread and butter, Spiced (oriental) salt. Finger bowl.

POTTED SHRIMPS. Cut brown bread and butter, cayenne pepper. Many guests appreciate lemon.

JUICES. *Tomato Juice* (*Jus de tomate*).
Worcester sauce on table (teaspoon for stirring).

FRUIT JUICES. For other fruit juices ensure that the caster sugar sifter (or similar dispenser) is available if required.

Fruit Appetisers

MELON (MELON AND CANTELOUPE). Two kinds of melon are frequently served. Canteloupe and Honeydew. The canteloupe is a yellow-skinned, gourdlike melon. Honeydew is a larger, usually greener of rugby football shape. Lay a cover for guests of a melon (fruit) knife and fork placed across the plate, the tip of the handle of the knife resting on the prongs of the fork. An optional addition may be a sweet spoon laid across the plate with its handle to the right. The slice of melon is normally placed on the plate at the side-board, in the space formed between the crossed knife and fork. It is then placed in front of the guest.

MELON ACCOMPANIMENTS: A silver flat with two bowls, one with caster sugar and one with ground ginger, is passed. In serving, place a couple of teaspoons of sugar neatly on the side of the plate and a smaller quantity of ginger alongside it, according to the guest's request. Sugar (or ginger) should not be sprinkled over the melon by the waiter. A sugar dredger should also be placed on the table when melon is served.

Melon is usually served as an hors d'oeuvre, but it can also be served as a sweet. Melon, especially canteloupe, is often made into a melon cocktail, flavoured with port or other wine. Parma ham is sometimes served with honeydew melon.

GRAPEFRUIT (*Pamplemousse*) AND FRUIT COCKTAIL (*Cocktail de Fruit*). Grapefruit are always prepared before the service and usually by the waiting staff. They are halved and then each segment of the flesh must be cut separately. The half grapefruit is served (usually decorated with a cocktail cherry) in a special silver cup placed on an entrée plate with a tea-spoon alongside the cup. It is served from the left.

GRAPEFRUIT ACCOMPANIMENTS: Fine caster sugar must be passed immediately the grapefruit has been served and left on the table. A finger bowl is to be passed afterwards.

The service of a fruit cocktail is similar except that they are served either in special cocktail coupes or in glasses. No finger bowls need be passed afterwards.

Entrée

Table setting or cover required for an entrée is a joint knife and fork and an entrée plate. An entrée is complete in itself and is therefore served on one silver dish, usually flat. A spoon and fork is the required service gear.

Macaroni, spaghetti, noodles (nouilles) and other pastes are also served on an entrée plate. The cover cutlery traditionally consists of a joint fork only, placed on the right hand side of the cover. But nowadays a dessert spoon (or even table spoon if not too large) is usually placed on the left. For omelets also a fork alone is traditionally placed on the right hand side.

Fish (Poisson)

When fish is covered with a sauce such as Mornay, Dugléré or Bonne Femme no preparation is required before serving. The waiter must, however, take care not to break the fish. He must see that each person is given a complete portion with adequate sauce and a helping of the steamed or boiled potato usually served.

When fish is fried, (meunière) or boiled, some preparation is required before serving. For a steak of fish, or "tronçon", the bone has to be removed and the outside skin peeled off with a spoon and fork, with care taken not to break up the flesh. Bones and skin removed must be placed on a separate plate and on no account be left on the dish as it is served.

In the case of a whole fish such as a Dover sole, usually served grilled or meunière, the small bones around the fish must be trimmed away. Each fillet is then lifted separately from the spine bone with a spoon and fork. Other types of sole are only trimmed off the small bone. The centre bone remains in the fish as it is nearly impossible to remove without breaking the fish.

When sole is deep fried, small bones are removed before cooking. Fillets may, then, be removed by the waiter two at a time. The centre bone is taken out and the fish is rebuilt on to the dish before serving.

As a general rule, salt water fish are served without the head while fresh water fish are served with the head still on.

All preparation of fish before serving must be done at the service table, or in the case of special dishes such as "truite au bleu", on a guéridon in front of the customer; but never on the customer's table.

COLD LOBSTER (*Homard Froid*). Fish knife and fork is laid at the guest's cover. Half a lobster is the usual portion. It

VII.
Private Function
Room in
Period Style

Traditional decor and furnishings are still favoured in many small banqueting suites in hotels and restaurants. In this room, with table laid for a private luncheon or dinner, furniture of the early 18th century French Regency period imparts an atmosphere of richness.

Behind the green marble-topped consol table, supported by kneeling blackamoors, the wall is covered with looking-glass panels. Flanking the gilt wall-clock, are slender black columns topped by gilded capitals. The chairs, in the comfortable Louis XVI style, are of Italian walnut upholstered in Chinese green.

**VIII.
Private Function
Room—
Modern Style**

Here is shown a private party lay-up in a modern idiom. Note the colourful uniforms of waiters from the London Hilton's International Restaurant.

is dressed in the shell on a silver flat on a bed of shredded lettuce. Usual garnish is half hard boiled egg, tomatoes and slices of cucumber. The dish is first presented to the guest, then it is brought back to the service table for preparing.

First, the waiter places a little shredded lettuce on the guest's plate. Then, using a spoon and fork, he lifts the flesh from the tail and cuts away the shell part of the tail, leaving the flesh attached to the body of the fish. He places this portion on top of the lettuce on the plate. Next, using a clean napkin he picks up the claw in his left hand. He breaks the shell of the claw in half (this has been cracked previously in the larder), and eases the flesh with the fork out of the shell. This too he places on the plate. Next he decorates the plate with the half hard boiled egg, tomato and cucumber. Having prepared all the plates in this way (when more than one person is being served with this) he places them in front of each guest.

COLD LOBSTER ACCOMPANIMENTS: Mayonnaise sauce is passed separately in a sauceboat. An oil and vinegar cruet can be placed on the table for this dish.

Fish Accompaniments

   Deep Fried (Egg and breadcrumbed) (frit à l'anglaise)—
   Tartare sauce, $\frac{1}{4}$ lemon.
   Deep Fried (in batter) (frit à l'orly)—Tomato sauce (hot
   or cold) lemon.
   Grilled (grillé)—Tartare or Hollandaise (or derivative),
   Maître d'hôtel (or anchovy or similar) butter.
   Poached (poché)—Hollandaise sauce, melted butter or egg
   sauce.

Poached fresh salmon (saumon poché)—Cucumber salad (salade de concombre), Hollandaise sauce.

Cold salmon (saumon froid)—Cucumber salad, mayonnaise.

Whitebait (blanchaille)—Cut brown bread and butter, lemon, cayenne pepper.

PARSLEY WITH FISH. Fresh parsley sprigs served with fish are intended to give colour and are not usually served by the waiter unless by request of the guest. But fried parsley is part of the dish and should be served.

Main Course

As a rule no preparation is required here except in special cases for à la carte dishes such as entrecôte, double Porterhouse steak, Chateaubriand, pheasant, grouse, etc. Service is straightforward, first the meat, then vegetables are passed and finally sauce from the sauceboat.

The waiter must take care to give each person an equal portion and, if the dish is decorated with vegetables, potatoes, watercress and so on, he must see that he serves some of each to every guest. French and English mustard are nearly always required with this course. They should be passed by the waiter and not just left on the table.

When clearing after this course, side plates are removed if no vegetable course follows and a sweet is next on the menu. Cruets, sauce bottles and other condiments are also cleared as well as toast melba and butter. When all is clear except for glasses, the table is crumbed using a folded napkin and a plate. Then the sweet spoons and forks are put on or brought down (whichever is house custom) and the sweet plates are put on.

Main Course Accompaniments

MEATS:

Roast lamb (Agneau rôti)—Mint sauce (sauce menthe) or jelly.

Roast saddle of mutton (Selle de mouton rôtie)—Red currant jelly or onion sauce.

Roast leg of mutton (Gigot de mouton rôti)—Red currant jelly or onion sauce.

Roast shoulder of mutton (Epaule de mouton rôtie)—Red currant jelly or onion sauce.

Boiled leg of mutton (Gigot de mouton bouilli)—Caper sauce (and puree of turnip).

Jugged hare (Civet de lièvre)—Red currant jelly.

Salmis of game (Salmis de gibier)—Red currant jelly.

Roast beef (Boeuf rôti)—Horseradish sauce, Yorkshire pudding.

Boiled salt beef (Silverside) (Gite à la noix)—Carrots, onions, dumplings.

Boiled, fresh beef (French style) (Boeuf bouilli à la française)—Grain or rock salt, gherkins, grated horseradish.

Braised ham (Jambon braisé)—Spinach (epinard), Madeira sauce (sauce Madère) or peach sauce.

Grilled ham (Jambon grillé) or boiled, baked ham—Appropriate sauce on menu as mustard, tomato, horse-radish.

Braised tongue (Langue de boeuf braisée)—Florentine garnish, spinach, Madeira sauce.

Roast pork (Porc rôti)—Sage and onion stuffing, apple sauce (demi-glace).

Roast veal (Veau rôti)—Savoury herb stuffing and bacon and brown sauce (jus lié).

Curries (Kari)—Boiled rice, chutney, papadums, Bombay duck. (Indian restaurants serve many other accompaniments).

Calf's head (Tête de veau) (hot)—Vinaigrette or Gribiche sauce. (Some of the brains may be mixed in the sauce before serving.)

Grills—Mustards (to be passed). Proprietary sauces (on table).

Cold meats (English buffet) (Assiette Anglaise)—Mustards, pickles, chutney, proprietary sauces, relishes.

Note: With beef, pork, ham, tongue, liver and kidneys, offer French and English mustard.

POULTRY AND GAME

Roast duck (Caneton rôti)—Sage and onion stuffing (farce aux oignons) apple sauce (sauce pommes), (roast gravy).

Roast goose (oie rôtie)—Sage and onion stuffing, apple sauce. Roast gravy.

Roast chicken (Poulet rôti)—Bread sauce, roast gravy (possibly also grilled bacon and sausage).

Roast turkey (Dindon rôti)—Cranberry sauce, savoury herb or chestnut stuffing, chestnuts, chipolatas.

Roast game:
Grouse
Partridge (Perdreau, Perdrix)   } Bread sauce, fried breadcrumbs, roast gravy.
Pheasant (Faisan)
Other game birds

Note: Game chips usually accompany all roast birds.

Vegetables

Vegetables, particularly the finer ones may be served as a separate course after the main one or quite commonly today, as an introductory course.

VEGETABLE ACCOMPANIMENTS:

Asparagus (Asperge) (hot)—Hollandaise sauce, melted butter.

Asparagus (cold)—Mayonnaise sauce, vinaigrette or Gribiche.

Artichoke (Artichaut) (Globe, hot)—Hollandaise, melted butter.

Artichoke, Globe (cold)—Mayonnaise, vinaigrette or Gribiche.

Beets (cold) Betterave—Vinaigrette.

Broccoli (Brocoli)—Hollandaise sauce.

Cauliflower (Choufleur)—Hollandaise, melted butter.

Corn on the cob (Maïs)—Melted butter.

Spinach (Epinard) (en branches)—Cream, sometimes veal gravy.

Salads

In restaurants offering high class service, it falls to the waiter to prepare dressings "in the room" and then to dress the salads before the guest. For small quantities this is often mixed on a plate or soup plate, e.g., by mixing by fork, mustard (French or English), a little pepper from the mill and salt with a little wine vinegar—then whisking in the oil.

Dressings, however elaborated, are then best blended with leaf salads in the bowl. Dressed salad may then be transferred to the crescent shaped salad plates which are placed together with a dessert fork by the top left-hand side of the guest's meat plate.

THE SERVICE OF SALADS. Salads should be placed on the table immediately before the rest of the course. The plates are placed at the top left (10 to 12 o'clock). The half moon or kidney plate should fit the meat plate just above the side plate. For cut salads a small fork should be placed on the plate. For heart salads a small knife and fork is required.

Certain fruit salads, for instance those served in an orange or apple, need a teaspoon.

When on the table, the salads should all look uniform in size, design and position. There may be difficulty in finding room for the last salad if they are not placed in the correct position. The cruet, the odd glass, can be moved to make room. Such items as ash-trays, menus, table numbers, water jugs, etc., may be removed from the table.

Sometimes a customer prefers to make his own dressing. In this case the salad bowl should be placed on the table above the couvert, the required ingredients at the top left, and a large plate with a large spoon and small fork, in front of the customer. When he has dressed his salad it may be removed, and arranged on the salad plates by the waiter.

SERVICE. Too often insufficient care is taken in the service of salad. It is wrongly relegated to a few lettuce leaves with a garnish of pieces of tomato, cucumber and beetroot. The service of salad is as important as the rest of the meal and gives the waiter scope to show his skill and willingness to give good service.

Types of Salad

In this country the following main types of salad are served:

LEAF SALAD: Lettuce leaves (round, i.e., cabbage lettuce or cos), corn salad, chicory, endive, watercress, can be mixed as a "composite" salad, or made individually as separate salads. Use Vinaigrette dressing (see Dressings below).

HEART SALAD: Good quality round or cos lettuce with a tight heart. Served in halves or quarters according to size.

Both these types are served with cold meats. They can also be served with game, or a grill on customers' request.

FRUIT: Chiefly used with game, or highly spiced or marinated dishes. Clean fruit flavour "cuts" the richness of the dish.

COLD COOKED VEGETABLES: Chiefly root (whole or sliced) arranged decoratively—carrots, turnips, onions, kohl-rabi, celery, celeriac, leeks, etc.

RAW VEGETABLE SALADS: Shredded turnips, carrots, cabbage, celery, chicory, celeriac, spring onions, kohl-rabi, etc.
These ingredients can be combined in any mixed salad to customer's wish and according to season. They can also be served separately as individual salads.

Salad Dressings

In general the English have a dry palate and are not fond of olive oil (corn oil and ground nut oil may be preferred). The French have a sweet palate and like olive oil. Americans, who are big salad eaters, have a sweet palate of a different nature. So dressings employed for salads should be balanced to appeal to customers palates. Some of the more popular dressings are:

FRENCH	Salt, pepper (mill), French mustard and one part vinegar to three parts oil.
ENGLISH	Salt, pepper, English mustard, and two parts vinegar to one of oil with caster sugar to taste. (The sugar is to "cut" the vinegar if too sharp for palate).
AMERICAN	Similar to English with equal oil and vinegar and sweetened with sugar.
MAYONNAISE	Mayonnaise sauce thinned with vinegar and lemon juice to a dressing consistency.

LEMON	Salt, pepper, fresh lemon juice and olive oil to taste, with caster sugar. (Very popular with people who do not like vinegar).
SAUCE VINAI-GRETTE	Salt, pepper, one part vinegar to two parts olive oil. (This dressing basis used also for certain hot dishes as with plain boiled calf's head). French or English mustard is often blended in additionally to guests' requirements.
SAUCE RAVIGOTTE	Vinaigrette with a heavy garnish of chopped chives, chervil, tarragon, capers and parsley.
SAUCE GRIBICHE	Mayonnaise dressing with a garnish of chopped gherkins, capers, chervil, tarragon, parsley, and strips of hard white of egg.
ACIDULATED CREAM	Fresh cream and fresh lemon juice seasoned with salt. Various other items are added according to salad. (Used mainly for the fruit-type salads.)
THOUSAND ISLAND	Mayonnaise dressing with a little chili sauce and chopped red pimento, chives and green peppers.

Method of Dressing Salads

At the appropriate time the salad should be presented and the customers asked if they would like it dressed and, if so, their taste. Salads, especially green salads, should never be dressed until the last moment or their crispness will be lost. On receiving sanction for dressing, the waiter mixes his dressing on a dinner or soup plate.

Measure out the salt, pepper, mustard (sugar) and vinegar and mix. Then add the oil. By moving the plate briskly back and forth with the left hand and whisking with a flat fork on the plate with the right, a creamy texture will form.

Never mix dressings in a silver sauce boat or dish: the article will be badly scratched and be ruined.

LEAF SALAD: Pour the dressing over the salad in the bowl and then remove the garnish on to a plate. With a spoon and fork lightly turn and twist the leaves in the bowl. This imparts a thin coating of dressing all over the leaves. Place the leaves neatly on salad plates and decorate with the garnish which is also dressed.

HEART SALAD: Care must be taken not to flood the salad with dressing. Lightly mask the open part with dressing, using a teaspoon, so that the dressing sinks between the leaves. Dress the garnish and arrange all on to the plates.

FRUIT-TYPE SALAD: Acidulated cream dressing is usually employed. Many such salads are already dressed, but some, where green salad is also used, need dressing at table. These salads should first be arranged on plates and then the fruit only lightly masked with the dressing.

Examples of Salads with Suggested Dressings

Archiduc	Julienne of beetroot, endives, truffle and potato—Vinaigrette.
Augustin	Heart of cos lettuce with French beans, quartered tomato and hard-boiled egg, and green peas—Mayonnaise.
Demi-Deuil	Heart of lettuce with strips of truffle and potato—Vinaigrette.
Eleonora	Heart of cos lettuce garnished with base of artichoke and asparagus points—Mayonnaise.
Eve	Scooped out apple filled with a dice of apple,

	pineapple and banana—Acidulated cream dressing.
Florida	Hearts of lettuce with quartered oranges—Acidulated cream.
Française	Lettuce leaves with quartered tomato and hard boiled egg, and sliced beetroot and cucumber—French.
Gauloise	Leaves of cos lettuce with strips of fresh nuts—Mayonnaise.
Legumes (de)	Diced potato with chopped French beans, green peas, and cauliflower—Vinaigrette.
Louisette	Heart of cos lettuce with quarters of tomato and skinned pipped grapes—Vinaigrette.
Lorette	Corn salad with strips of beetroot and celery root—Vinaigrette.
Niçoise	French beans, quartered tomato, sliced potato, decorated with fillets of anchovy, olives and capers—Vinaigrette.
Rachel	Strips of celery and truffle, base of artichoke, potato and asparagus points—Mayonnaise.

Sweet

At lunch time, cold sweets are usually presented on a trolley when service resembles that from hors d'oeuvre trolleys. The waiter wheels the trolley round the table and serves each guest individually according to the guest's instructions.

For hot sweets, hot plates are used and placed before guests. The waiter holds the serving dish on his left hand and serves the sweet with a spoon and fork or a spoon only according to the type of sweet.

For sweets served in "coupe", the coupe is placed on the sweet plate with a teaspoon alongside it on the plate. For ice cream, wafers are passed separately. They must be neatly arranged on a silver flat with a doyley, and never be stuck in the ice cream. If a customer, after taking a trolley sweet orders at the same time another sweet which is served in a coupe, then the waiter spoons the sweet from the coupe to serve by the side of the other sweet on the same plate.

Cheese and Biscuits

A clean side plate and side knife are placed in front of each guest. A fresh dish of butter pats served on an under-plate with a fork alongside is placed in the centre of the table. A dish or plate with a doyley containing a selection of biscuits such as cream crackers, is placed on the table. (Whole tins are sometimes presented, either wrapped in a napkin or in a specially made silver container). Then the waiter presents the cheeses, on a cheese board, to each customer, cutting a piece of the selected cheese with a special knife and placing it on the customer's plate. A glass containing sticks of celery is also placed on the table. Watercress may also be made available.

Savouries

For this course and when dealing with modern cutlery, a joint knife and fork are used. A hot plate is put in front of each guest. A plate covered with a folded napkin carrying salt and pepper, pepper mill, red pepper and Worcestershire sauce is placed on the table. Other sauces may be added to this according to the nature of savoury. In some cases French and English mustard may appropriately be passed.

Fresh Fruits

A finger bowl half filled with tepid water is placed on a fruit plate, a fruit fork to the left and a fruit knife to the

right also on the same plate. The tip of the knife must rest
on the prongs of the fork. The whole cover is placed in front
of the guest and the finger bowl is lifted and placed above
the plate by the waiter. This movement is done on the left
of the customer.

The fruit basket is then presented to the customer from
the left. The waiter carries the basket of fruit on his left
hand. In his right hand he holds a pair of scissors. If the
customer wishes an apple, an orange, a pear, etc., he helps
himself from the basket. If the guest wishes grapes, the
waiter cuts the stalk with his grape scissors, dips the grapes
in a bowl of cold water, which he also carries (placing it on
the table while serving the customer). He serves the small
bunch of grapes on to the customer's plate with the help of
the grape scissors.

Service of Coffee

This service is dealt with in Chapter 12 on Breakfast, Tea
and Coffee.

Presenting the Bill

The waiter must always check his bill before presentation to
ensure that it is correct. Shortages have already been mentioned and the management abhor over-charging. It is
detrimental to the good name of the establishment.

Bills can be paid in two ways. Either by the customer to
the waiter to the cashier, or by the customer on leaving, direct
to the cash desk (house custom).

The bill should first be folded from bottom to top with
the right-hand corner (the corner opposite the total, so that
the total is not revealed) turned back, then placed on a cash
tray or plate. The time for presenting the bill varies with
the type of restaurant. In a quick-service restaurant, after

the waiter has ensured that the party requires nothing else, he can usually place the bill on the table at the left-hand of the host, but in the more leisurely restaurant more service may be required after the meal, so the bill must remain open until asked for. No time should be lost in presenting the bill once it has been demanded. At no time should a waiter give the impression that he is trying to get rid of his customer —either because other guests need the table or because the restaurant is nearly empty and he wants to get home.

The bill with the money should be taken to the restaurant cashier for encashment and the receipted bill with the change on the plate should be placed on the table at the left-hand side of the host. When giving the change, also on the plate or salver, the waiter must not wait around for a tip even if the customer does not collect his change off the plate immediately. When the customer eventually takes his change, the waiter should not remove the plate with the tip until the customer has left the table, unless the guest expresses in some way the desire for the plate to be removed.

Any tip left on the plate, of no matter what size, should be picked up graciously with the plate with a "thank you very much, sir".

When the guest rises from the table in order to leave, the waiter must immediately come forward and help the guest to put on his coat, to hand him his hat and gloves, etc. He must also check that nothing belonging to the customer has fallen under the table or is hidden under the napkin. If the tip is still on the plate, the waiter must thank the customer sufficiently clearly for him to hear, whatever the amount, just when he is ready to leave.

11

Waiting Basics in Banqueting

The success of a banquet depends largely on its preliminary organisation. Each waiter taking part must similarly organise himself and his own section to fulfil adequately his own role in the function.

Pre-Banquet Organisation

It will help him to know something of the arrangements which precede the banquet as well as those which apply during it.

The following departments require prior notification of the function: Kitchen, restaurant (Banqueting or Function Manager), cellar, house-keeper, hall porter, still-room, plate room.

Apart from the usual "special business sheet" normally sent to all departments each week, further forms giving all necessary information to departments concerned may also be sent from the manager's office a few days in advance of the function. Kitchen and waiting staff require the following information:

Kitchen

1. Date and time of function.
2. Number of services required and number of covers per service. (This information is supplied by the Function Headwaiter).

3. Any other information which may be required from the service point of view.

Restaurant (Banqueting Manager or Function Headwaiter)

Date and time of function and;

1. Number of covers to be served.
2. Where to assemble.
3. Where to serve.
4. Details of the menu.
5. Plan of the tables.
6. List of guests.
7 Drinks, aperitifs: wines, liqueurs, spirits, and whether pre-ordered (booked) or cash.
8. Cigars, cigarettes.
9. Any other information.

Factors affecting the above numbered points include:

1. NUMBER OF COVERS. This is usually the number of guests expected and it may not be the number who will be present. As it is difficult, if not impossible, to add covers at the time of the function without disorganising both kitchen and service, an accurate estimate must be received.

2. WHERE TO ASSEMBLE. The aperitifs and Zakouskis are served in a reception room. A few chairs should be placed around the walls, so that elderly ladies may sit down. Small tables, with ashtrays, for the guests to deposit their empty glasses, must be provided.

3. WHERE TO SERVE. This information is supplied with the table plan.

4. DETAILS OF THE MENU. This consists of the menu for
    the actual function in the room, and also information in
    case Zakouskis have to be served during the reception,
    and tea, sandwiches and cakes later on during the even-
    ing. Soup on departure may also be required or, in
    certain cases, breakfast.

5. TABLE PLAN. It is usual procedure in a large hotel
    catering for all sorts of functions to have ready three or
    four alternative standard seating plans for each one of
    the rooms used for this type of business. It is advis-
    able to ask organisers to select one of those plans instead
    of using one of their own, This is because in arranging
    seating the organiser forgets to take into account such
    factors as doors, windows, pillars, which affect the
    service. The "house" table plans referred to as A, B,
    C and D and so on must all have been tested; either by
    careful calculation and planning or by actually putting
    the tables in position. The various sizes of the banquet-
    ing tables and of the cloths must be taken into considera-
    tion when drawing up a plan.

    One or two copies of the table plan must be displayed
    for the guests in the reception room. For a large func-
    tion, each table on the plan will carry either a letter or a
    number. Beside this plan a list of guests in alphabetical
    order indicates where the guest is seated by letter or
    number. Only in special circumstances are actual seats
    numbered at table, other than the top table. At the top
    table, each guest is informed of his place, usually by a
    name card at his (or her) seat. This information is pre-
    viously advised by the organisers.

DRINKS. Wines, aperitifs and other drinks can either be
paid for by those giving the function or paid for by each

individual guest. In the first case there are two alternatives. Either the organiser may order beforehand what drinks are to be served and how many bottles, or each guest may order what he wants. The guest will sign the checks as well as the waiter serving the drinks.

In the second case, the guest orders whatever he wants and pays for it himself. This is referred to as "cash drinks". A limited wine list is often used for this type of business.

As for the aperitifs, it is not uncommon for organisers of functions to decide that a limited number of glasses will be paid for by them (usually one for each guest) and the rest to be on the cash basis.

A special reception bar is usually provided for a function of any size so as to facilitate the service. It is set up in or near the room where the reception is being held, with a barman or a wine waiter in charge. Stock for this bar is drawn directly from the cellars.

Liqueurs and spirits can also be obtained, and these again can be paid for by the organiser or by individual customers.

The function headwaiter must be informed as to what time a special licence, if any, has been obtained for this function. He is responsible for seeing that no drinks are served after the time limit has expired.

Cigars and cigarettes are sometimes provided by the organisers themselves and handed to the headwaiter at the time of the function. These can also be ordered by the organisers when the function is first booked, in which case, the function headwaiter will have to be notified. He may then draw his requirements on the morning of the function from the stores. Cigars are passed round in boxes by the wine waiters at a large function or by the function headwaiter at a small one. Cigarettes in glasses or boxes (a dozen or so in each) are placed at intervals on tables after the Loyal Toast (of the Queen).

OTHER INFORMATION. Sometimes a function organiser asks the headwaiter to check on numbers present at the function and to notify him of that number as soon as possible during the meal.

The number of waiters or waitresses required both for the service of the drinks and food will have to be decided well in advance. A usual quota is one food waiter for each ten guests and one wine waiter for each twenty-five guests.

If an announcer or toastmaster is required for the reception or for the dinner, a toast list will have to be provided for the announcer.

Instructions to Plate Room

The plate room must be notified in advance of the date, time and place and total numbers attending the function. It is, however, advisable to give greater details to this department. They have to attend not only to the supply of silver for the kitchen but also to plates and cutlery and glasses.

They will, therefore, require to know details of menu, number of services required, how many on each service, or better still the sizes and types of silver for each course, if finger bowls are required, if special glasses must be made available to the glass pantry and any other information to suit the particular occasion.

Instructions to Still Room

This department requires only information to provide adequately for rolls, butter, toast melba, coffee and milk. All they generally need to know is date, time, place and total number.

On certain occasions, however, tea, sandwiches and cakes or breakfast may be served later on during the evening or early hours of the morning. Then, the still-room will need advance notification as they, as well as larder department, attend to this requirement. A complete detail of what is wanted must be given.

Reception and Preliminaries
Reception

It is customary for a banquet to be preceded by a cocktail reception for which some of the function waiters may be required. The cocktails usually are gin and French vermouth with a stoned olive on a cocktail stick, (dry martini); gin and Italian vermouth with a cocktail cherry on a stick (sweet martini). Glasses of sherry make up the choice of drinks offered to the guests. In certain cases other drinks can be obtained on demand. Zakouskis (small, savoury appetisers) with items such as cheese straws, game chips, salted peanuts, cocktail onions, are arranged in small dishes around the reception room on small tables for the guests to help themselves. Zakouskis, however, are sometimes handed round by the waiters. Half an hour is normally allowed for the reception.

The table plan is usually displayed in the reception room to afford a guest maximum advance notice of where he is sitting.

On receiving the signal from the organiser or chairman, the toastmaster or announcer bangs his gavel three times and says, "Mr. Chairman, My Lords (or other titles in order of importance), Ladies and Gentlemen, dinner (or lunch) is served", in a loud, clear and formal tone of voice.

Dining Room Preliminaries

The doors of the banqueting hall are opened and guests take their seats at table. In some cases, top table guests do not enter the banqueting hall until all other guests have found their places. Then the announcer will add, when announcing the dinner, "With the exception of the top table, will guests kindly proceed to the banqueting hall". On such occasions, all guests in the room stand when the top table guests come in and will only resume their seat when everyone at the top table is seated.

During these preliminaries, waiting staff stand to attention at their respective stations.

The announcer now calls guests to attention by banging three times with the mallet saying "Mr. Chairman, My Lords, Ladies and Gentlemen, pray silence for the Reverend So-and-So, (or Mr. So-and-So), who will say grace".

Once this has been done, the meal begins.

Mise en Place

As a banquet success hinges upon its organisation, a complete mise-en-place of all material required is essential.

All cutlery must be on the table or on the waiter's service sideboard. This latter applies, for example, to fruit knives and forks for dessert which are not set on the table until they are required. The various wine glasses that are going to be used must also be on the top table; except liqueur and brandy glasses which remain on the wine service sideboard until required.

Place Setting

Cutlery and covers are laid as for table d'hôte dinner (though usually a full range is required) but there are two ways in which glasses can be arranged:

1. In a straight line across the top of the joint knife in the order in which they are going to be used, starting from

the right with the sherry glass and finishing with the port glass.

2.   In the form of a triangle, the sherry glass being the pivot. Glasses to be used first are placed to the right, others to the left.

Space and Guests per Waiter

The guests have been seated by the table plan according to the room's size, shape and number to be accommodated. This plan allows a minimum space of four and a half feet between each table for the chairs and a space wide enough for the waiter to be able to serve.

Banqueting tables may vary in size as they are usually made to individual specification, but they usually accommodate three to six guests on either side. The space required for each cover is 28 inch minimum to 32 inch maximum. The waiter may, therefore, have to work in a limited area.

Banquet Service

A banquet menu usually has five or more courses. Each waiter allocated a number of covers varying from eight to 12 according to the function's importance. A wine waiter may serve up to 30 or 35 covers. The function headwaiter and the toastmaster or announcer normally stand behind the chairman during the meal and during the speeches following the meal.

Timing and Movement

Waiters clear and serve together as a well drilled team. During the service of the meal all staff movements are directed by the function headwaiter. He gives necessary signals to the waiter serving the Chairman to begin serving or clearing. It is, therefore, of the utmost importance that other waiters when not actually serving, stand at the foot of their stations constantly keeping an eye on the top table as well as their own station. They must not lean against walls, pillars or furniture. On no account must they enter into conversation with one another.

Wine waiters, however, enjoy greater freedom of movement. They have to go in and out of the room for their customers' orders when drinks are on a cash sales basis. When wines are pre-booked, wine waiters receive one or two bottles of wine each of the first one to be served. They do not receive more of that wine, or of any other wines to be served, unless they return the first bottles they have received whether empty or not. Control on wines hinges on the fresh bottles being supplied only on the return of an equal number of empty or partly empty ones.

Toast Procedures

At the conclusion of the meal when the coffee cups have been placed in front of the guests, the toastmaster again calls the guests to attention with his gavel. He announces, "My Lords, Ladies and Gentlemen, pray silence for your chairman who will propose the Loyal Toast". As soon as this has been done, ashtrays must be placed on tables by the wine waiters. This toast is also an indication that the formal part of the meal is over and guests are now allowed to smoke. When coffee has been served (immediately after the loyal toast), the food waiters have their coffee pots and milk jugs refilled. After a reasonable length of time, coffee is passed again. After this the coffee cups are cleared and the food waiters leave the room for good. Wine waiters only now remain.

Speeches and replies follow from time to time each being

announced by the toast master in the usual manner, "Mr. Chairman, My Lord (if any) Ladies and Gentlemen, pray silence for Mr. So-and-So, who will propose the toast . . . ." (of the Association, for example) or "who will give the reply. . . . ."

During this time the wine waiters move quietly amongst the tables serving drinks. Glasses must never be empty during this period of toasting. They must change ashtrays frequently (covering the used ashtray with the inverted clean one, removing both together and replacing with the clean). Under no circumstances should a waiter go round with a plate on which merely to empty dirty ashtrays. At this stage, wine waiters have taken over from the food waiters. They complete all the service that is required by the guests.

Specimen Banquet Menus

The following three menus not only indicate the type of menus served at banquets but also illustrate the sequence and build-up of a meal and its courses as outlined in the section on menu composition in Chapter 4

BANQUET

———

Huîtres impériales d'Ostende
Consommé des viveurs en tasse

———

Langouste froide à la parisienne

———

Mignon de boeuf favorite

———

Neige au Champagne

———

Poularde de Bruxelles dorée
à la broche
Salade Lorette

———

Surprise d'Hawai

———

Mignardises

———

Moka

———

Magnums G. H. Mumm Cordon Rouge 1937

BANQUET DE CLOTURE DU Ier CONGRÈS

DE L'ASSOCIATION INTERNATIONALE

DE L'HOTELLERIE AU PRÉ CATELAN

(PARIS 1947)

Germiny

———

Délices de sole Walewska

———

Pouilly Fuissê

Château Mouton Rothschild 1933

Noisette de pré-salé
Pré Catelan

———

Château Haut-Brion 1934

La Romanée Conti 1937

Perdreau rôti sur canapé
Pommes chips

———

Château d' Yquem 1937

Salade Lorette

———

Champagne

Cognac—Liqueurs

Glace Armenonville
Mignardises

———

Fruits de France

———

Café

BANQUET IN THE GRAND STYLE

---

les huîtres impériales
ou
les joyaux de la Volga en barquette
Persryba - Malossol

Gewurztraminer-vieille chapelle
1937 le bisque d'écrevisses

---

les oeufs "Zingara"

---

la truite de la Lesse aux amandes grillées

---

château Calon Ségur, mise le médaillon de veau à la Chimay
du château, 1939 pommes Dauphine

---

les primeurs de lamines flots d'or

Musigny 1939 le délice de foie gras de Strasbourg au porto

---

magnum Pommery brui,
1929 les oranges glacées, givre de la citadelle

---

la tarte namuroise

---

le moka "Casino"

12

Serving Breakfast, Tea and Coffee

General rules of mise en place and of meal service apply to the serving of breakfasts and beverages but sometimes the importance of these in creating a favourable impression on the guest may be overshadowed in the waiter's mind by the gastronomic interest of luncheons, dinners and banquets. It would be most unfortunate if waiters and waitresses should fail to give especially careful attention to the service of breakfasts and the "national" beverages tea and coffee.

Breakfast Mise en Place

Two types of breakfast are served in hotels; the plain or Continental breakfast and the full or English breakfast. A plain breakfast consists of tea or coffee, rolls, toast, butter and marmalade. In some hotels brioches and croissant are also available.

The full English breakfast is, indeed, a more elaborate meal and requires more preparation in the dining room before service than other meals. Grapefruits are to be cut (this must never be done the previous night), and oranges squeezed. In some cases all the various cereals, jugs of cream and of cold milk, are arranged on a table (usually cold buffet table) in the dining room. Services of jam, honey and marmalade are to be prepared. Jugs of iced water and a supply of glasses are "en place" on each sideboard.

EXAMPLE OF A FULL ENGLISH BREAKFAST MENU:

Grapefruit
Fruit juice (orange, lemon, pineapple, etc.)
Tomato juice
Stewed fruits (plums, apples, figs, prunes, etc.)

———

Porridge or cereals

———

Steamed fillet of Haddock
Fried fillet of Sole
Grilled Herring
Kedgeree

———

Fried Egg and Bacon
Poached Egg on Toast
Grilled Sausage and Fried Egg
Mushrooms on Toast
Grilled Kidneys and Bacon
Grilled Tomatoes

———

Fresh Fruits
(oranges, apples, pears, bananas)

———

Marmalade, honey, preserves

———

Toasts, brioches, croissant, rolls, brown bread

———

Tea, Coffee, Milk, Chocolate

Tables also require much preparation as more items are set on them than at any other meal. In order, therefore, to be ready on time for breakfast service, as much as possible of the mise en place is done the previous night.

Previous Evening's Preparation

The evening before, therefore, a clean tablecloth is laid on the table then the cover is set. A full breakfast cover consists of a medium sized plate, a joint knife and a fish knife to the right, a joint fork and a fish fork to the left. In front, a sweet fork, handle to the left and a sweet spoon, handle to the right. On the left hand side of this, a side plate with a side knife on the right edge of the plate, in line with the other cutlery. A slop basin, a set of cruet and an ashtray are positioned symetrically on the table.

Next morning, table settings are completed with: breakfast size cups and saucers (placed beside the tip of the fish knife), tea spoons, table napkins (placed square on the medium size plate.) A bowl of soft and one of lump sugar are then placed on each table, together with a jug of cold milk, a jug of cream, and a service of preserves (marmalade, honey and jam—often in miniature jars). This mise en place is done by the waiters.

During this same time, commis attends to sideboards, stacking up cutlery, plates, cups, saucers, napkins, large and small tablecloths, and anything that may be required during service. Commis also prepare grapefruits, orange juice, grapefruit juice, tomato juice, etc., and jugs of iced water. Condiments for commis to assemble include fresh mustard, Worcestershire sauce, bottles of vinegar, etc.

Anything not required for breakfast should never be brought into the room nor kept on the sideboard. Unnecessary items will only hinder the waiter during service. Floral decorations are seldom used for breakfast.

Breakfast Service

The breakfast menus are presented to each guest by the section headwaiter or station waiter and the order taken in the usual manner (Chapter 8). Instructions given by the customer regarding the preparation of his order (timing of egg, etc.) must be written on the check.

The service of this meal is fundamentally the same as for any other meal. The commis brings dishes from the various departments to the sideboard. The waiter verifies the correctness of the order and then serves it to the customer. First class service of breakfast is done on silver, but many hotels have adopted plate service for breakfast in order to expedite service. For plate service, the waiter usually collects orders from the kitchen and his commis attends to requirements from the still room.

Coffee, toast, hot rolls, brioches and croissants are placed on the table at the same time as porridge or cereals unless a guest stipulates otherwise.

At breakfast time toasts are always served in a toast rack. It must never be laid flat on a plate or served in a pile. This makes it soggy and unfit to be served. Always see that tea and toast are freshly made and coffee and hot milk really hot. Remember customers rightly blame the waiter if they are not; for whether or not he caused the fault he is certainly responsible for checking that items are freshly made and hot.

When the waiter clears away the plate used for the main course, he must remove any spare (i.e., unused) silver left on the table. He also moves the side plate directly in front of the guest. Similarly he moves the toast rack and service of marmalade and preserves nearer the customer. The waiter must then ask if more toast, coffee or a fresh pot of tea is required.

Needless to say, the customer must never be kept unnecessarily waiting between courses. If there is any delay in food service, the delay must be referred to the section headwaiter. He should investigate and seek to remedy any service hold-up and at once inform the guest, regretting the delay and explaining he is seeking to overcome it.

Floor Service Breakfasts

This is done by floor waiters. Trays and trolleys are used. (See Chapter 9, page 107, re tray setting). They are laid with china and cutlery the previous night in the floor pantry. At the last minute the waiter places the hot food and beverage on the tray or trolley and takes it to the customers at the requested time.

Floor breakfasts are usually ordered the previous night or given as a standing order.

After knocking at the guest's door and waiting to be admitted, the tray is placed either on a special side table (only on the bed if the guest asks for it). If a trolley is used, it is wheeled into the room and placed either in the centre, by the window or by the bed at the request of the guest. Usually trays are used for single orders and trolleys for an order for two persons.

The dishes brought are then shown to the guest in case the order is incorrect or not to his liking. It can then be changed without the guests having to ring for the waiter again.

When the waiter is about to leave, he must ask if anything else is required, otherwise he will not enter the room again unless he is called for. Often the tray or trolley is left for the chamber maid to clear when she is cleaning the room. She will place it either in the passage or in the floor pantry for the waiter to clear later. Ordinarily he will send dirty plates down the lift but retain cutlery, pots and cups to wash himself. These latter are usually his stock and he must keep them in his pantry.

For this reason the floor pantry must be equipped with a sink, a lift to the still room and the kitchen, facilities for boiling water and keeping coffee and milk hot. Normally a telephone or a speaking tube is connected to the kitchen and the stillroom. In some cases, tea and coffee are obtained from the stillroom with the other part of the order, but usually dry tea and a supply of hot coffee and milk are sent up to the floor pantry.

Check books for floor service are usually marked "floor" and are of a different colour from the other departments (dining room, etc.). Room numbers must be carefully and clearly marked as an extra charge is customarily made for floor service.

Duplicate checks, bills, etc., must be passed on to the cashier as soon as possible, as customers often leave immediately after breakfast.

Tea Making and Service

Tea is such an important beverage in Britain that every good caterer takes the greatest care to make it and serve it in the best possible way.

The Still Room (Cafeterie)

Although in many establishments tea is made by a stillroom maid or service counterhand and the waiter is concerned with serving it, the following details are given because the information should be of use to him.

It must, in any case, be born in mind that the stillroom where tea, coffee and similar beverages are prepared, traditionally comes under the supervision of the restaurant manager or maître d'hôtel rather than the chef de cuisine. In this department are similarly prepared toasts (plain and melba), butter pats and, often, sandwiches at times of larder closure.

Making Tea

Tea should normally be made and served in teapots. Nothing else achieves the standard of perfection that is desirable. The best type for making tea is an earthenware pot, with a non-drip spout. Silver or plated pots are also suitable but care must be taken that they are thoroughly cleaned and dried after use, otherwise they will tend to become stained and musty. For making tea in large quantities stainless steel pots are recommended, although it is recognised that bulk brewing of tea is necessary for rapid service to very large numbers.

There are five golden rules of tea-making:

1. USE GOOD TEA. High quality blends produce better tea.

   USE FRESHLY-DRAWN, FRESHLY-BOILED WATER. Water easily goes "stale" if allowed to stand, and water that has been boiled before should never be used again for tea-making. Again, water which has not come to the boil causes tea to be flat and insipid.

3. WARM THE POT. If water is poured into a cold pot, it will go off the boil and the tea will not be so good.

4. USE THE "SHORT POUR". To get the full benefit, the water should reach the tea leaves as near boiling point as possible. If kettles are being used, the rule is: take the teapot to the kettle, and not the kettle to the teapot. If, as is more likely, a boiler is being used, then make sure the teapots are brought right up to the boiling water outlet.

5. TEA SHOULD BE BREWED NOT STEWED. The time to be allowed for infusion should be between four and six minutes, depending upon the size of the pot and the nature of the water. The larger the pot, the longer the time for infusion: soft water infuses tea more readily than hard.

If the tea is being served in cups, it is advisable to put the tea in the cup before the milk is added. However hurried the service, the milk should never be put in the teapot or urn.

Quantity to Use

Tea should always be used in measured quantities: this is the only sound rule for economy and for good tea-making. For teapot service one teaspoonful of tea is required for each half-pint of water, which approximates to the sound rule: One teaspoonful of tea per person, plus one teaspoonful for the pot. However, several types of tea-measuring machines are on the market for stillroom and canteen use. For large-scale tea-making, scales are necessary to measure the exact quantity the establishment stipulates.

When large teapots are used and where there may be some danger of the tea "standing" and becoming over-infused, it is desirable to use an infuser. This should be made of monelmetal gauze or electro-tinned copper, having the finest possible perforations which should not be less than 225 to the square inch.

Storage of Tea

Tea should be kept in a dry, cool place and away from strong-smelling commodities such as soap, fruit, cheese, spices and disinfectants which can quickly affect its flavour.

If bought in packets, the tea should be kept in a box with the lid closed. If in a chest, this should be raised off the floor and kept away from walls, to allow a free current of air to pass under and around.

When teapots with separate lids are not in use they should be cleaned and dried or stored upside down with the lids off, so that the moisture can drain away and the teapot be kept "sweet". Those with hinged lids, such as silver teapots, should be cleaned and dried thoroughly, and then stored with the lids closed.

Large Scale Tea Service

There will be special occasions when the caterer is called upon to supply tea to many hundreds of people, all of whom may require service at about the same moment. In this case the multipot, so extensively used for industrial tea services, is the best method. These receptacles are really like giant vacuum flasks in that they enable tea to be stored and kept at piping hot temperatures for any time up to four hours. This means that the tea can be brewed well in advance of the peak period. These multipots are constructed with linings of stainless steel which, if kept clean, do not in any way affect the flavour of the tea. They are lagged with heat-retaining materials and have an outer casing of polished stainless steel, chromium-plated copper or stove-enamelled tinned steel.

When used, they should, like teapots, be thoroughly warmed inside; the leaf tea is then put into the perforated metal infuser supplied as part of the multipot. The inside should be filled to the top with boiling water, otherwise the air space left will lower the temperature of the stored contents. The infuser should be removed after 10 to 15 minutes, but before withdrawal it should be vigorously agitated to ensure that all of its contents have been in contact with the boiling water. After withdrawal the infuser should be gently tapped with the hand to dislodge leaves, but not banged, as the metal is easily dented.

Wherever possible tea should first be put in the cups, the milk added and the customers allowed to take their own sugar. If, however, it is essential to make the whole mixture in the urn, draw off some tea and add sugar to the rest in the form of a syrup. Add milk at the last possible moment.

Urns and multipots should be cleaned immediately after use. Taps must be cleaned daily. When not in use the utensils should be stored upside down with lids off and taps open.

Coffee Making and Service

At breakfast, coffee, milk and sugar should be placed on the table in a coffee jug, milk jug and sugar bowl. Customers should help themselves in the same way as in their own homes. If several people of one family occupy a table, the coffee service should be placed on the right of the eldest lady present.

Coffee served after luncheon or dinner should be served by the waiter.

Prior to coffee service, the table is once again cleared and crumbed, all the guests having finished eating. Dirty and empty glasses are removed, but glasses not emptied must not be removed without the guest's consent. In some cases, a small, clean white cloth is laid on the table to cover any stains which may have been made during the service of the meal. A clean ashtray is then placed on the table.

A small coffee cup and saucer should be placed on a china plate with the coffee spoon at an angle so that the handle points to the customer's right hand. This service is placed from the left in front of each guest.

The waiter carries a coffee pot, milk jug and sugar bowl on a plate with doyley or tray with doyley or cloth on the palm of the left hand. The waiter must make sure that the coffee and milk are really hot. He should go to the right of the guest and enquire "Will you have black coffee, sir, or with milk?" He will then enquire, "Do you take sugar, please sir?" and if so, "How many lumps?" (or spoonfuls if brown, for example, is the guest's choice). The cup can then be filled with coffee to a quarter inch from the brim. First, he serves the coffee by tilting the pot without lifting it from the silver flat; then he does the same with the milk jug if required. Alternatively, sugar can be served separately first and the bowl left on the table.

It is preferable not to refer to coffee as "white" for this is a slang expression. In any case it is not always understood by visitors from overseas.

In the best service the coffee pot is inclined in a downwards position, making a pivot of the part of the pot exactly under the spout, but in such a way that this pivotal point does not leave the tray or plate. This requires a little practice. (Plate

V illustrates this method).   When the service is completed, coffee pot and milk jug are placed on the table at the host's right.

Liqueurs

Liqueurs are usually served into the glass and carried on a silver salver to the table, then placed at the right of the coffee cup, but not near the edge of the table. This procedure is appropriately varied if there is a liqueur trolley service in the room.

Tea in place of Coffee

If a pot of tea is required by a guest, a small tea cup, teaspoon and saucer, on a side plate are placed in front of him. A small tray carrying tea pot, hot water jug, milk jug, is placed at his right-hand side to permit the guest to help himself whenever he judges that the tea is sufficiently infused. Tea is never poured into the cup by the waiter.

Coffee Making

As the stillroom links with waiting staff, it is useful that the fundamentals of coffee making be understood. But additionally coffee is often infused in the restaurant itself by filters, percolaters and patent devices. If certain rules are adhered to, the making of good coffee is a simple procedure. Coffee should be strong without being bitter, of a dark but bright colour and full flavoured with a pleasant aroma.

There are varied appliances for coffee making, but to obtain a balanced coffee, coffee should always be freshly made, never more than a half hour or so before serving.

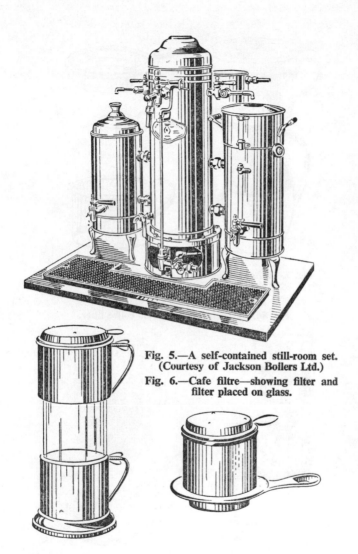

Fig. 5.—A self-contained still-room set. (Courtesy of Jackson Boilers Ltd.)

Fig. 6.—Cafe filtre—showing filter and filter placed on glass.

Fig. 7.—Filter Coffee Pot (Courtesy of T. Collinson &
Sons Ltd.)
Fig. 8.—The Cona coffee machine.
Fig. 8a.—French fireproof china coffee filter.

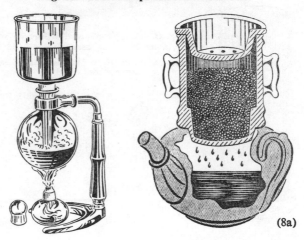

(8a)

Coffee kept hot too long or reheated loses its bright fresh colour and flavour. The appliance employed should always be thoroughly clean. Coffee takes other flavours very easily. Good maintenance of apparatus is an essential factor. The same blend of coffee should always be used and at the correct grind for the machine. The ground coffee must always be weighed or measured to balance with the amount of finished liquid coffee required. Guess-work can cause the flavour to fluctuate from meal to meal and cause complaints. A very approximate guide is 8 oz. of medium ground coffee to one gallon of water.

Coffee in making or when being kept hot must never boil or even simmer. Boiling will extract the caffeine and other harsh qualities and cause the coffee to become bitter. Although boiling water is used in making coffee the apparatus is so designed that the temperature drops to just below boiling (about 208°F.) before infusion with the grind. Made coffee is usually kept at about 180°F. for service. The pots and cups should be heated before serving to ensure that the customers do not get tepid coffee. If fresh cream is preferred to milk it should be poured gently on to the coffee so that it floats on top.

Making Coffee in Quantity

Most large establishments use coffee machines making one or two gallons at a time (see diagram on page 157) and if used correctly these make very appetising coffee. It is usually made by the still-room maid.

Individual Coffee Making

Some customers like their coffee made at the table to ensure it being fresh or because they require a special type of coffee.

There are various types of machine which are used, the most popular in this country being those illustrated on pages 157 and 158.

Vacuum Infusion Method (heat-resisting glass)

A diagram of the apparatus is shown on page 158. This method is very simple to use and makes perfect coffee if employed correctly. The correct measure of medium-grind coffee (one heaped teaspoon to each small coffee cup to full capacity of the bowl) is placed in the funnel which has already the glass stopper in position. The bowl is filled to one inch from the top with boiling water. The funnel is fixed firmly into the bowl with a slight twist to ensure that the join is airtight and the lighted methylated lamp placed underneath. The boiling water will be forced up the funnel tube and infuse with the coffee grounds. It should be left up for one minute. If some of the grind does not mix it can be lightly stirred, but great care must be taken not to touch the stopper. The lamp is then removed and the coffee will descend into the bowl. If the descent is retarded it will be because of an airlock, in which case it can be cleared by placing the lamp under again and sending the coffee back up, giving a slight extra twist to the cork and allowing the coffee to descend again. When all the coffee has dropped into the bowl the funnel is removed (with a reverse twist) and the coffee served from the bowl in the normal way. For full efficiency the machines should always be used to capacity. As they are made in various sizes, if the correct size is used this is a simple matter.

Electric Simmerstat Method

Many establishments are now using 3-pint machines in

batteries in strategic positions in the room for the regular coffee supply. The machines work on the same principle as the table models, but can be made ready slightly in advance of service and kept at the correct temperature by controlled heat.

Filter Method

On the Continent the method mostly employed for individual coffee is by the filter or drip method. There are various appliances, all basically the same (see diagram on page 157). They consist of a filter funnel in which the coffee is placed, which fits on top of the pot, glass, or cup, and through which the coffee slowly percolates.

Wines, Drinks, Licensing and Tobacco

Fine wine deserves proper care, storage and service. It is, therefore, essential for a wine waiter to know the conditions that should prevail in the cellar and the manner in which the various wines should be served.

Storage

The cellar should, if possible, be underground and away from the main thoroughfare, in order to minimise the risk of vibration. The average cellar temperature should be 55°F. Bottled wine, when once binned, should not be disturbed until it is required for service: therefore, each type and vintage must be stored separately, with each section of the binning space correctly numbered to facilitate easy location of the wine; these numbers should correspond with those on the wine list.

In cellars where red and white wines have to be stored in the same room, the red wines should be in the upper bins or warmer temperature and the white in the lower or cooler temperature. Continual changes of temperature should be avoided, otherwise the condition of the wines will be materially affected.

Types of Glasses

Wine is appreciated by its colour, aroma and taste, and the

shape and type of the glass used helps considerably to bring out these characteristics.

A wine-glass should be of good clear glass. It should be curved at the top so that the "nose" (aroma) is trapped and the nose can appreciate the bouquet. The glass should be thin so that the lips can help the palate to enjoy the flavour of the wine. Thick glassware definitely spoils the pleasures to be found in wine-drinking.

Many establishments have now adopted a standard size of glass (6 oz.–8 oz.) for all table wines. The tulip shape is most favoured; it has an approximate capacity of six glasses per bottle of wine.

Champagne glasses (of the "coupe", saucer or fluted shape) are still widely used for their particular purpose. Good brandy is served in large balloon glasses in many establishments.

Setting Glasses on the Table

During the general setting of the room, the wine waiter will be responsible for placing an all-purpose goblet at each cover. These goblets are carried upside down between the fingers of the left hand. The method of loading and unloading glasses carried in this way is very important as it can cause a great deal of breakages if it is not properly carried out.

Waiters should train themselves at an early stage to carry glasses in this way as it is a quicker and safer way of transferring them from the pantry shelf to the tables. Tumblers must always be carried on salvers.

During the service of the meal, however, glasses must always be carried right way up on salvers (round trays 12 inches in diameter, having a concave edge) whether they are being taken to or removed from a table. The waiter places the glass on the table at the right side of the cover at the outside tip of the large knife; or if there is not a large knife, then just where it would normally be placed. Tables are usually laid with a standard wine glass. If it is necessary to change it, the fresh glass should be brought on the salver to the table and the glasses exchanged by picking up the table glass on to the tray and placing the fresh glass in its place on the table.

Glasses should always be removed from the table when empty. Fresh wines (even if a second bottle of the same wine is ordered) and other drinks should always be served in fresh glasses. They should at all times be handled by the stem (between thumb and fingers), or for the tumbler type, low down near the base. Glasses must never be picked up or cleared by putting the fingers inside. Clean glasses should only be brought into the room during service when they are required so that they can go straight on to the table. Dirty glasses should be removed on a salver or tray and, as they come off the tables, should be taken to the glass pantry. They should always be carried on their own and never placed out of sight under a sideboard. Broken glass in a room can be very dangerous; too much caution, therefore, cannot be exercised in the handling of glassware.

When laying banqueting covers, three or more glasses, e.g., sherry, claret and/or hock and champagne should be placed in the order of use, with the smallest glass to the right. Above them on the table should be placed a port glass and a liqueur glass.

Glass Commonly Used for Wine and Drink Service Include:

Water or wine goblets	Capacity,	8 oz.
Claret glass	„	6 oz.
Sherry glass	„	3 to 4 oz.
Port glass	„	4 oz.

Liqueur glass	Capacity usually very small.
Hock glass	Tulip shape, usually amber coloured, long stem.
Moselle glass	Tulip shape, usually green coloured, long stem.
Burgundy balloon	Very large glass for fine burgundy wines.
Champagne tulip	Tall, slender glass.
Champagne coupe or saucer	Straight side, very wide at top. (Traditional but not now fashionable).
Cocktail glass	Varies in shape.
Lager glass	May be tall, flute type or stemmed "hock" type.
Brandy balloon	Large glass with a narrow opening and a short stem.

Other containers include:

Jugs for water and beer.

Silver or pewter tankards in ½ pint (and, possibly, 1 pint measure) for draught beer and bottled beer other than lager.

Ordering Wine

The sale of wines in licensed restaurants is always profitable. For the high class restaurant it is a "must" as a meal is not complete without wine. Therefore, the wine list should be presented at each table at the proper time—that is, when the food order has been given. But it is just as important for the wine to be served correctly.

The waiter should present the wine list from the left-hand side of the customer, and when the order has been given he should write out a cellar check. This is usually made out with two carbon copies; the original is sent to the cellar or dispense in order to obtain the bottle, the duplicate is given to the cashier and the third copy is handed to the station waiter for reference and comparison with the bill when it is presented for payment. As we have seen, wines are ordered by numbers in most establishments. In the wine list, to the right of the description of the wine, are two columns showing the price of whole and half bottles. Thus the check illustrated below, for an order taken by waiter W.O., would read 1×57 or $\frac{1}{2} \times 57$ according to the customer's requirements, the price being altered accordingly.

When the bottle has been obtained, the waiter should present it to the customer, from the latter's right-hand side, at a suitable angle so that he can easily read the label, and mention the name of the wine and vintage, if any, for example, "Your Château Latour 1953, sir". Care should be

	Table No.
	15
1 x 57	
	140p.
Date 9/4/70	Sig. W.O.

taken not to shake the wine (for this may disturb any sediment) or to shake any dust from the bottle on the table.

When the customer has approved the wine, the waiter should leave the table, remove any wax, or cut the tinfoil round the lip, carefully wipe the lip of the bottle (or some sediment may drop in the glass later), and draw the cork. The best corkscrew for the wine waiter is the lever or the French Boxwood corkscrew. Correct use allows the cork to be drawn quietly and smoothly with no fear of breaking the neck of the bottle. The screw should not be driven right through the cork or pieces may fall into the wine. The cork

should be pulled to within a quarter to half an inch of the
end and then withdrawn with a slight twist by the thumb and
fingers. This allays any last minute jerk of the bottle and
allows the air to take the place of the cork more steadily.
(In no circumstances should the waiter hold the bottle between his legs when drawing the cork).

He should then cover the forefinger of his right hand with
the corner of a waiter's (clean) cloth, insert it in the opening
of the neck of the bottle (meanwhile holding the bottle
steady in the left hand), and gently wipe inside, in case there
is any vestige of cork there (see Figs. 9 and 10). The wine
may now be served.

Serving the Wine

The waiter should first pour a little wine into the host's glass;
the latter should sample the wine to satisfy himself that it is
in good condition and suitable to serve. When it has been
approved, the waiter should continue serving the wine to the
guests, beginning at the right of the host with the ladies,
then from the right again with the gentlemen until the host
is reached and the service thereby completed.

Wine should be poured carefully and steadily. The bottle
should be held (label uppermost so that it can be read) with
the hand over the bottle, the thumb round one side, the
fingers round the other and the index finger lying up the
shoulder (not on the neck). The lip of the bottle should be
placed just over the edge of the glass and then tipped downwards with a movement of the wrist until the wine begins to
flow. In this way the pouring is under complete control and
can be stopped at will by just moving the hand upwards again
by pivoting from the wrist. At the end of each pouring
possible drips can be removed by touching the lip of the
bottle with a waiter's cloth folded into a pad.

Fig. 9.—Wine—opening the bottle.—The corkscrew should go nearly through the cork. If this is not done the bottle neck may break, a bottle of wine be lost and hands may be cut. Note clean napkin round bottle.

Fig. 10.—Wine—pouring into glass.—When held in
this position the bottle is properly balanced. Note the
position of the first finger, well back from the neck of
the bottle.

Corky Wines

Before serving a wine, the waiter should smell the cork carefully and if he detects any unpleasant odour, indicating that
the cork has gone musty and the mustiness has been absorbed
by the wine, he should at once either replace the bottle by
another or report the fact to the head waiter or manager.
Incidentally, most good wine shippers or merchants will replace such corky bottles.

Special Points in the Service of White Wines

White wines should be served slightly chilled at about 50°F.
Modern equipment allows most cellars to have the wines at
correct temperatures for service, but in some cases this is

not so, or the customer himself likes his wine colder. The wine can then be placed in a wine cooler with water and ice just to the shoulder of the bottle. The wine cooler can be placed in a stand at the side of the table, or on a large plate (on which has been placed a napkin), which can be placed on the table. Wine coolers are, however, intended mainly for keeping cool the remainder of the wine after the first service. A deeper receptacle is essential for the proper cooling of a bottle of white or sparkling wine. After presentation, with the aid of a lever screw the cork can be removed without taking the wine from the cooler. When offering the host the sample to taste, ask if the temperature of the wine is satisfactory. If the answer is that it is not cool enough, the host should be asked if he would like a little to be poured out at the moment or if he would prefer all the wine to be returned to the cooler for another few minutes. Similarly, when the wine has been served the host should be asked if he would like the wine which has been left in the bottle replaced in the cooler or left out as it may now be chilled sufficiently. Care must be taken that wine is not over-iced for the aroma of the wine can then deteriorate.

With white wines, no more than two-thirds of a glass should be poured. When placing a bottle on the table it should be put just above and to the left of the host's wine glass, with the label facing him. The wine waiter should keep a constant contact and refill the glasses when necessary. When the bottle is empty he should politely inform the host that the wine is finished. The host can then order more wine if he thinks fit.

A napkin should be placed at the wine cooler for the purpose of wiping the bottle each time it is taken out. This napkin must not, however, be used for wiping the neck of the bottle when serving the wine.

Special Points in the Service of Red Wines

Red wines should be served at room temperature—about 65°F. Most establishments do their best to have sufficient red wine stored near the room for this purpose.

Old red wines have a sediment and therefore must be handled very carefully, or this sediment will be disturbed and make the wine thick. It is better that they be decanted in the cellar to allow of the least possible disturbance. For these very old reds, the wine waiter should, on receiving the order, recommend decanting. On some wine lists it is stated that all red wines over a certain age will be decanted unless the customer wishes otherwise. The wine waiter should then politely point this out to save repercussions if the customer is offended through having his wine opened before presentation.

Before serving such decanted wine, the waiter should present the original bottle and cork to the customer to assure him that the wine he has chosen is, in fact, being served. Should a customer insist on the wine being served from the bottle, the cellarman will place the bottle in a wine cradle; the cork will be drawn only after the bottle has been presented at the table. The lever corkscrew is of great value in removing corks from bottles in cradle. The corks can be very soft and crumbly after so many years and great care must be taken in the opening.

Heavy decanters are generally used for old port wine, whereas other wines are decanted into more delicate carafes so that their colour may be fully appreciated.

Should the customer complain that the wine is not "roomed" and he requires it "chambré" (French for roomed) on no account should the wine waiter immerse the bottle in hot water, stand it in front of a fire, or place it on a hot-plate. Such drastic action will kill the fine quality and bouquet of the wine, and send it cloudy. As the only safe method is to raise the temperature gradually, the head waiter should be informed. If the customer insists that something be done, the least drastic method is to warm a decanter and carefully pour in the wine so that it gathers the warmth as it fills. In residential hotels an astute wine waiter will get to know his guests and take wine orders during the previous meal, so that red wines can be placed in the room well in advance. Another great point in favour of this is that the cork can be drawn to allow the wine to breathe. This assists an old red wine, for it has been imprisoned for a long time. The younger red wines have not had time to gain a sediment, but although they do not need decanting they should be handled with grace, as indeed should all wines.

The quantity poured should not be more than half a glass to allow the aromas to expand and the bouquet to be enjoyed.

Champagne and Other Sparkling Wines

Sparkling wines are served chilled. They are often appreciated more chilled than the still white wines. After presentation, not forgetting to mention vintage (if any), the cork may be drawn.

The wire is removed at the point indicated on the gold foil (generally a piece of twisted wire). The cork is then removed with the right hand, by a slight twisting movement, the bottle being held in the left hand. The waiter should have quick access to the host's glass, or the wine will surge out of the bottle and "fizz over". By near access to the glass the bottle neck can be quickly inclined over the glass, and the wine and fizz can go into it instead of being spilt. The cork should then be smelt for "cork" before the other guests are served.

If the bottle is "corky", the host's glass can then be removed, with the bottle, and another substituted.

A cloth should be placed over the hand gripping the bottle while the cork is extracted. Champagne bottles should be handled gently. Agitation of the bottle before opening causes increased effervescence, i.e. "fizz", which impedes good service. Do not allow the bottle to point in the guests' direction when drawing the cork.

Sequence of Serving the Different Kinds of Wines

The correct classification of wines as served with the various courses is as follows:

Graves or Chablis	With Oysters.
Sherry, Marsala, Madeira ..	„ Soup.
Hock, Moselle, Sauterne, or Chablis	„ Fish.
Claret, Burgundy, Chianti or Champagne	„ Relevé or Entrées
	„ Roasts and Entremets.
Port	„ Cheese.
Port or Malaga	„ Fruit.
Brandy and Liqueurs	„ Coffee or later.

The custom of serving a different wine with each course is not, however, observed nowadays, except on formal occasions. The present-day fashion is that a sherry is served with the soup course, after which any one of the table wines mentioned above will be served with the remainder of the meal.

Generally speaking, dry wines come first and sweet wines last; if a dry wine is served after a sweet wine it will taste too dry (i.e., sour), whereas the sweet wine, coming after the dry, will taste sweeter and more agreeable.

Some Useful Hints to Wine Waiters

Never recommend a wine unless you know its qualities.

Never cool a wine by placing ice in the glass.

Never use soap or soda when cleaning a decanter, but use warm water and small lead shot, or raw potatoes diced, and allow the decanter to dry before using it again.

Always keep stoppers off decanters after they have been washed in order to allow the inside to dry thoroughly.

Always use clean glasses when serving a second bottle of the same kind of wine.

Always wash glasses in hot water, rinsing in hot, and then polishing with a glass cloth.

A glass should not only be clean, but beautifully clean.

When in doubt remember that:

Dry wines are served before sweet wines.

Young wines are served before old wines.

White wines are served before red wines.

Some of the Principal Wines

FRENCH

Champagne		Produced from the district around Rheims.
Bordeaux	Red.	Usually known in England as Claret.
	White.	Graves, Sauterne, Barsac and their types.
Burgundy	Red.	Burgundy, Côte d'Or, Beaujolais, etc.
	White.	Chablis, Pouilly, Meursault, etc.
Cotes du Rhône	Red.	Burgundy type.
ALSATIAN	White.	Moselle type.

GERMAN
| Hock | White. Rhine Wine. |
| Moselle | White. Moselle. |

SPANISH

Sherry — Derives its name from the town of Jerez.

Also many dry table
    wines.

PORTUGUESE
| Port | River Douro. |
| Madeira | Island of Madeira. |

ITALIAN
Chianti	Tuscany.
Capri	Island of Capri.
Asti	Sparkling. Piedmont.
Lacrimae Christi, etc.	Naples and southern Italy.

EMPIRE

Australia and South Africa produce red and white wines which are similar to claret, port, hock, burgundy and sherry.

There are also various types of wine emanating from Hungary, Austria, Jugoslavia, Greece, Russia (Black Sea).

The Service of Other Drinks

The Appetiser

The appetiser is enjoyed before a meal to set the palate working, and is usually partaken of in the lounges or bars, but in the restaurant the customer often likes one at the table. Therefore, on seating a party, the host should first be asked if he would like a sherry, cocktail, or other appetiser. These should be served as quickly as possible so that they can be enjoyed even whilst the order for the meal is being taken.

Sherries, in general, are classified as "dry", "medium" or "sweet", although they are often asked for by name. Some visitors have a preference for Dubonnet, Madeira, Marsala, or other sweeter aperitif wines. The waiter should know the ingredients of a few of the more popular cocktails to assist him in taking an order. As these drinks are served in the glass they should be carried on a cloth-covered wine salver in case of slight spillage during carriage. If the base of the glass is wet on arrival at the table it can easily be cleared by rubbing a finger off the base on to the cloth. Picking up a filled glass to wipe it can cause more spillage and possible accident. It is easier to change the cloth on the tray if it gets soiled. The glass should be placed on the table just below and to the right of the table glass, which should not be removed. When the drinks are finished the glasses should be cleared.

Some Common Cocktails

The mixing of cocktails is a task for the trained and qualified barman. A waiter, who may find himself on lounge service or assisting at a pre-function reception, should, nevertheless, know the ingredients of a few commonly demanded cocktails. These include:

Bacardi	Rum, lime juice, sugar, Grenadine.
Bloody Mary	Vodka, tomato juice, lemon juice, Worcester sauce, salt, pepper
Brandy sour	Brandy, lemon juice, sugar, cherry garnish
Champagne cocktail	Champagne, brandy, bitters, lemon peel
Daiquiri	As Bacardi (without Grenadine)
Gin and Dubonnet	Gin with Dubonnet aperitif wine

Gin and Italian	Gin with Italian vermouth
Gin and French	Gin with French vermouth
Manhattan	Rye whisky, Italian vermouth, bitters
Martini (dry)	Gin, French vermouth, olive garnish
Martini (sweet)	Gin, Italian vermouth, cocktail cherry garnish
Old Fashioned	Whisky, bitters, sugar, fruit garnish
On-the-Rocks	Any liquor served neat poured over ice cubes
Rob Roy	Scotch whisky, Italian vermouth, bitters
Screwdriver	Vodka and orange juice on ice cubes
Sidecar	Brandy, Cointreau, lemon juice
Whisky Sour	Whisky, lemon juice, sugar, cherry garnish
White Lady	Gin, Cointreau, lemon juice

Service of Beers

Bottled beers are usually served from half pint (10 oz.) bottles
and poured into a 12 oz. glass. They are served with a
"head" or "collar" (froth) and there should be no delay in
serving so that there is still a full "head". English beers are
served at normal temperature. Lager beers (including English) are always served chilled. Draught beers served in half
pints or pints must be served in glasses, mugs or tankards
bearing the official crown marking and quantity, and must
be full to this mark.

Liqueurs

Are served in glasses which vary in size and shape according
to the preference of the establishment. They have a line cut

into the glass to mark the measure. The bottles should be taken to the table, presented, and the measure poured into the glass in front of the customer.

Liqueurs originated in Roman times, but were more fully developed by the monks in the Middle Ages, when they experimented with distillations of herbs, flowers and grape juice (brandy). These ancient recipes were used as medicines; the secrets being passed down through the generations, so that the ingredients of many of the better known liqueurs of today are still closely guarded secrets of the monasteries after which the liqueurs are named. Many of the properties in liqueurs are of great assistance to digestion and so the partaking of a liqueur after a meal became a popular feature. In modern times the industry has grown and many liqueurs, mainly with a fruit basis, have been invented and placed on the market.

Some Liqueurs and Their Predominant Flavours

Abricotine	Apricot
Advocaat	Yolks of egg and brandy
Anisette	Aniseed
Apry	Apricot
Aurum	Orange
Benedictine	Herbs and brandy (D.O.M.)
Calvados	Applejack brandy
Chartreuse	Herbs (137) brandy (Green or Yellow)
Cointreau	Orange (White)
Crème de Cacao	Chocolate (with fresh cream on top)
Crème de Menthe	Peppermint (Green, White)
Curaçao	Orange (Yellow, Green, White and Blue)

Drambuie	Herbs and Scotch whisky liqueur
Glen Mist	Irish whiskey liqueur
Goldvasser (Danzig)	White spirit, herbs and gold leaf
Grand Marnier	Orange
Izarra	Mountain herbs and brandy (Basque)
Kirsch (Wasser)	Cherry kernels (bitter almond)
Kummel	Caraway seed
Tia Maria	Coffee and rum
Trapestine	Herbs and brandy (Abbaye Grace de Dieu)
Van der Hum	Herbs, bark, tangerine-orange
Vieille Cure	Herbs and brandy (Abbaye Cenon)

Service of Liqueur Brandies

Many gentlemen prefer a liqueur brandy after their meal. Brandy is a distillation from grapes. The freshly distilled brandy is very raw, fiery and colourless. It gets its mellow flavour and straw colour from years of maturation in cask. Spirit, unlike wine, does not mature in the bottle. As it is a spirit there is constant evaporation and therefore loss of stock. This, added to the fact that during the years it is lying in cask it means money which cannot be used, explains why there is so much difference in the prices of the various brandies. In general, the longer the brandy is in the cask the more mellow it becomes. Brandy is made all over the world, but that made in France is reputed to be the best. The finest brandy comes from Cognac, a defined area in France, and only brandy made in this area can be called Cognac.

As brandy is enjoyed as much by the nose as the palate it is usually served in a brandy goblet. The large bowl (balloon) allows the glass to be wrapped in the hands to warm it through and release the aromas. The narrow neck traps these aromas in the bowl and lets the nose gain full appreciation. When brandy is served—whether in a "balloon" or liqueur glass—the name, and possibly the vintage, should be quoted, for example, "Your Bisquit Dubouché, sir/madam".

As stated, a slight warming is necessary to release the aromas. There is a practice of warming the glass before putting in the brandy; indeed some customers ask for their glass to be warmed. This should never be done without the permission of the customer. Regular brandy drinkers usually prefer to use their hands, for if the glass is too warm the aromas can be released too quickly and the brandy somewhat spoiled. If, however, a customer requires his glass warmed, it should never be put over a methylated flame. Brandy is very delicate, takes in ulterior flavours easily, and can quickly gain the smell of the methylated from a contaminated glass. To warm a glass hot water should be used, afterwards wiping and polishing the glass thoroughly before pouring in the brandy.

On the other hand, in certain European countries the goblets are iced before the brandy is poured in.

NOTE: There are distillations made with other fruits and labelled "Brandy"; Cherry Brandy, Apricot Brandy, Peach Brandy, Prunelle (Plum Brandy) etc. These are liqueurs, not pure brandies and are served as liqueurs.

The Service of Spirits

Although spirits are more popular in bars, they are often ordered at the table instead of wine, and taken with mineral water.

WHISKY: Scotch, Irish, Rye, Bourbon.
Scotch whisky is preferred in this country, but Americans and Canadians have a liking for their own types of Rye and Bourbon.

GIN: "London Dry" of various brands is the most popular. Other gins include "Plymouth", "Hollands", "Sloe".

BRANDY: Served as a long drink with soda water is usually a younger brandy than that listed as a liqueur brandy.

Spirits are usually served by measure, the customer ordering a "Single" or a "Double". Many people demand a certain brand which, if in stock, should be served, but if not available the customer should be informed and an alternative offered.

The most usual mineral waters asked for with spirits are:

Whisky—Soda water, or similar aerated water, ginger ale, or plain water (which should be iced).
Gin—Tonic water and slice of lemon, ginger ale, ginger beer, or plain iced water.
Brandy—Similar to whisky.

Service

The waiter checks his order and obtains the spirits in glass and bottled mineral from the dispense. He then carries the order to the table—glasses and bottles on a wine salver. The glasses are placed on the table (see page 163) and asking the customer, "Would you say when, please, sir/madam", the waiter steadily pours in the mineral until told to stop. The mineral bottle is placed on the table if there is anything left in it.

NOTE: Ice should always be available as many people, especially Americans, like their spirits chilled when drunk in this fashion.

Service of Soft Drinks

SQUASHES:

Orange, Lemon, etc.: Bottled Squashes.

Place the measure of squash in the glass with ice and fill up with water, or soda water, giving a light stir to mix properly. Drinking straws in a stand or in a glass should be placed on the table at time of service.

Fresh Fruit Squash: (e.g., Lemon):

This should be made at the table. In preparation, place on a wine salver the freshly squeezed juice in glass (tumbler), a bowl of caster sugar, a bowl of ice, and straw stand, and then carry to the table with the soda water. At the table put in the sugar to customers' taste and dissolve into the juice. Add the ice and then slowly pour in the soda water, stirring lightly. Remember to make certain the sugar is dissolved and that the soda is added carefully, or there is liable to be an uncontrollable effervescence.

Mineral Waters

There are two types of mineral water: (1) Natural spring waters, which are bottled waters from the spas—some of the better known being, Vichy Etat, Vittel, Contrexeville, Evian, Perrier, Malvern and Apollinaris. (2) Manufactured mineral waters such as soda water, ginger ale, ginger beer, tonic water, lemonade, bitter lemon, etc.

For service, a quantity is poured into the table glass and the rest placed on the table in the correct position.

Licensing Law Affecting Waiters' Work

A waiter is not expected to know all the details of licensing law, but he should understand how it is applied to his work. As ignorance of the law does not excuse breaking it, a careless waiter could unwittingly jeopardise his employer's licence.

Application of the law has tended to differ according to types of establishment, but since the Licensing Act of 1961, changes have been introduced, to clarify licensing law and to eliminate anomalies. Differences still exist, however, between England, Wales and Scotland.

The type of licence held by an establishment is useful as a guide. Thus:

Hotels holding a full licence

(a) *Resident guests:* can be supplied with alcoholic drinks at any time of the day or night, with or without a meal. Payment for these drinks can be made at time of service, or be added to the guest's hotel bill. A resident guest can also obtain drinks for his personal guests at any time, providing he pays for these drinks himself. It is illegal for non-resident guests to order or to pay for alcoholic drinks outside Licensing Hours, even if they are in the company of a resident guest.

(b) *Non-resident guests:* can only obtain drinks during permitted hours. Drinks with a meal must be ordered during these hours. Up to thirty minutes after permitted hours are allowed for their consumption. If the drinks do not accompany a meal, only ten minutes "drinking time" is allowed. At the end of these times, it is advisable for the waiter to request permission to remove the glasses. This must be done with tact, particularly if foreign guests are involved, as they are often unaware of the Law.

Hotels holding a residential licence

In such establishments only resident guests can be supplied
with alcoholic drinks with or without a meal. No specific
times are laid down as to when these drinks can be supplied.
Personal guests of resident guests can be served with alcoholic drinks, providing these are ordered and paid for by
the resident guests.

Restaurant licence (sometimes called Table licence)

Drinks in this case can only be supplied if they are to accompany a meal. Drinks must be ordered during permitted
hours, and up to thirty minutes are allowed after permitted
hours for their consumption.

Some establishments have a licence combining the facilities
offered by the licences as in 2 and 3 above. In England and
Wales this is called Residential and Restaurant Licence (or
in Scotland a Restricted Hotel Certificate).

Restaurant holding a full-on licence. (Public-house certificate in Scotland)

Service of alcoholic drinks must take place during permitted
hours. They can be supplied with or without a meal, and
the customary drinking times after permitted hours are
allowed.

Unlicensed restaurants

These establishments cannot under any circumstances sell
alcoholic beverages, It is, however, permitted for Manage-
ments to allow their staff to fetch and carry for their diners
drinks obtained from licensed premises, for consumption

with a meal in their establishment. In this instance, certain conditions must be fulfilled.

A. The drinks must be obtained during permitted hours.

B. The guest must pay for the drinks when ordering.

C. The Management must not derive any revenue whatsoever for this service.

D. The Management is not allowed to hold stocks or alcoholic beverages for selling to customers.

In other words it must be a non-profit making service introduced purely for the convenience of customers.

Establishments holding a full licence or restaurant or residential and restaurant licence, serving meals late in the evening often have a Supper licence. This also allows them to sell alcoholic drinks for an extra thirty minutes after permitted hours at lunch time until 3 p.m. (2.30 p.m. in Scotland on Sundays) from Monday to Saturday as well as for an additional hour in the evening after permitted hours on every day of the week. These extensions only apply to drinks served with a meal, and thirty minutes consumption time is allowed in addition. The meal during the extension period, must be one of a "sustaining nature". Unfortunately, it is not yet clearly established, what a meal of a "sustaining nature" should be: That knives and forks are used does not in itself determine whether the meal is sustaining.

The main factor appears to be that drinks are an accompaniment to a meal rather than the meal an excuse for drinking. This applies to establishments which can only supply alcoholic beverages with a meal.

Sunday drinking

Only establishments holding a seven day licence can supply

alcoholic drinks on Sunday. The hours on this day differ from those applicable during the week.

Licensing Terms Defined

LICENSING OR PERMITTED HOURS:

The *general* licensing laws in England are:

Weekdays   11.0 a.m.—3.0 p.m.   5.30—10.30 p.m.
(11 p.m. in London).

Sundays   12.0—2.0 p.m.   7.0—10.30 p.m.

Local licensing justices have power to vary these times but permitted hours must not start before 10.0 a.m. nor end after 10.30 (or 11.0 p.m. in London). There must be a break of at least two hours in the afternoon and total permitted hours must not exceed 9 (or $9\frac{1}{2}$) hours.

In Scotland the hours are standard.
Weekdays: 11 a.m.—2.30 p.m. and 5 p.m.—10 p.m.
Sunday: 12.30 p.m.—2.30 p.m. and 6.30 p.m.—10 p.m.

Only Hotels and Restaurants can hold a seven day licence in Scotland.
Restaurant licence (table licence). Indicates that drinks can only be supplied with a meal.

SPECIAL LICENCE.   A permission valid for one occasion only, granted for serving drinks outwith permitted hours (i.e., functions) in the licensee's own premises, or for serving drinks during or outwith permitted hours in some other place. Only a licensee can be given this permission, and he must indicate date, time and place and reason on the application.

SUPPER LICENCE.   An extension of thirty minutes after closing time at mid-day during the week, and of one hour after closing in the evening for all days of the week including Sunday. During these extensions drinks can only be supplied with a meal.

AGE FOR SERVING OR CONSUMING ALCOHOLIC DRINKS. The permitted age for consumption of alcoholic beverages is 18. Persons under 18 but over 16 can be supplied with beer, porter, cider or perry to accompany a meal.

No person under the age of 18 can be allowed to dispense alcoholic beverages, nor be directly concerned with their service.

Tobacco

Customers nearly always order a brand of cigarettes or tobacco that they know and like. It is only with cigars that the waiter has often to recommend a particular brand.

The following sections apply to all tobacco, whether in cigarettes, for pipes or as cigars.

Purchase

Hotels and restaurants usually buy tobacco from wholesale tobacconists (tobacco merchants, cigar merchants, etc.), or direct from manufacturers of particular brands (although this will entail extra work, for more than one manufacturer's brands will have to be stocked).

Licences

An Excise licence to sell tobacco is no longer required.

Storage

Reliable merchants will make sure that all tobacco they sell to the hotel or restaurant has been stored properly up to the date of sale. Tobacco is sensitive and will easily absorb moisture like a sponge and even take on any strong smell near it.

Tobacco should not be exposed to extremes of heat or cold, or to wet or particularly dry air; otherwise the aroma is soon lost (particularly of cigars). A temperature of 65°F. is the most suitable.

Sale

As the customer nearly always knows what brand of cigarettes or tobacco he wants it is only necessary to stock a sufficient quantity of the more popular brands. Those that are in less demand should be kept only in such a quantity that they are sure to be sold before they lose their freshness.

Wherever a large quantity of tobacco (in any form) is sold, the hotel or restaurant will almost certainly have one member of the staff who is responsible for ordering, storage, sale, records and passing of invoices. The work of the waiter is then restricted to taking the customer's order, obtaining the quantity required, and seeing that it is properly paid for. In this case the method will vary; in many establishments the waiter will give in a special order to whoever is in charge of tobacco and obtain it in a similar manner to his obtaining food from the kitchen; he will then enter the item on the customer's bill. In others, and in most canteens, the customer is either required to pay cash at the tobacco kiosk or over the counter, or if the waiter takes the order he asks for the money and pays for it himself, without any record being made on his own check book.

The main types of tobacco for cigarettes and pipe-smoking are:

VIRGINIAN. By far the most popular. Grown in Virginia, the Carolinas, Kentucky and Tennessee.

TURKISH. From Asiatic Turkey, Balkans and Syria.

EGYPTIAN. From Nile Delta and Asia Minor.

RHODESIAN, and British Empire (particularly for pipe-tobacco).

Matches and Offering "a Light"

The waiter will remember that it is part of his duty to see that an ashtray (properly cleaned) is placed on the table for the guest at the right time and that a light (match, not lighter) is available should it be needed. If the guest asks for a "light" for a cigarette the waiter should strike the match (holding it away from the customer) and hold the flame to the cigarette. For a cigar, he will hand him the box of matches. The waiter should also have ready a cigar cutter. Connoisseurs of cigars prefer a cut end (either a deep V cut or straight slice) rather than a pierced end. The good "flue" provided by the cut ensures a cool, free drawing of the smoke, whereas a pierced end tends to become "tarry".

Choice of Cigars

The quality of a cigar depends on the tobacco. The best cigars are those which come from the Vuelta Abajo district, Number 1, in Cuba, where the tobacco is more aromatic in flavour than in any other part of the world.

Cigar smokers have different tastes. The majority like cigars to be mild. The "strength" of a cigar is determined by the "filler", which is the tobacco that makes up the main part of the cigar, and around which the "wrapper" or outer leaf is rolled.

The blenders, therefore, make all cigars of a particular

brand as uniform as possible. The mild and delicate blends are made of the finest and ripest leaf, but the full-flavoured ones are made of the heavier leaf which has the maximum of body and aroma.

Cigars are made in many parts of the world; e.g., Havana, Java, Jamaica, India, Burma, Manilla and Mexico. Some excellent cigars are made in Britain but they are, of course, from tobacco that is imported from Havana, Jamaica, Brazil, Java and America. Often the wrappers are leaf from Sumatra or Borneo, although Havana wrappers are also used on some brands.

A dark wrapper does not necessarily indicate a strong cigar, and both light and dark wrappers may be bitter and strong if the tobacco has not been properly ripened and cured by the highly technical processes employed. Proper maturing takes from six months to three years. Some cigars are graded by the colour of the wrapper (e.g., Claro (light), Colorado Claro (a little darker than Claro), and Colorado, which means "darker still").

Among brands of cigars sold in Britain, the leading ones are made in different sizes and shapes to suit individual preferences, e.g., Churchills, Lonsdales, Corona, Petit Corona, Half-a-Corona, Panatellas, Margaritas.

Although knowledge of what constitutes a good cigar cannot be given in a brief chapter, the waiter should bear in mind the following points, in addition to the fundamental data previously given:

(1) The ash of the cigar is some indication of its quality. A first grade cigar will produce a firm, greyish ash which will last for a considerable time before falling.

(2) It is not wise to put a cigar to the ear and to crackle it, because, although this will indicate whether it is dry

(which is most important) the crackling may break the leaf and damage the cigar.

(3) Cigars are usually sold in boxes of 25, 50, and 100. Cabinets are also provided, containing any number from 250 to 1,000, usually in assorted sizes.

(4) An attractive box or band does not necessarily mean a good cigar. Neither does, in fact, the wrapper of the cigar necessarily indicate that the more important filler is of equal quality.

(5) It is a good plan to keep cigars in a service cabinet, in which there is, say, a choice of three to six sizes, ranging from the good, moderate priced cigar up to the more exclusive and higher priced ones. A guest should then be able to make a suitable choice.

(6) A good cigar depends first and foremost on "reputation", which indicates the quality of the tobacco in the filler and wrapper, its correct maturing, grading, rolling, storing and packing.

14

Checking, Control and the Bill

As in all businesses, a checking system in hotels and restaurants is an essential part of the organisation. It is only by control—which implies checking at every stage—that food and drink can be properly co-ordinated in a short space of time with the aim of presenting a correct bill to each customer without delay.

Basically, as we have seen in previous chapters, all items— be they table d'hôte or à la carte dishes, wines, liqueurs, tobacco, or coffee—have only been obtained by a waiter on the presentation of a check (or voucher) for the articles required.

This checking—fundamentally the same in all establishments—naturally varies in detail according to the circumstances of the house and the type of business for which it caters. A check is written proof that the customer has been served with the items he has ordered, and if a dispute arises the mistake (if any) can be adjusted and the waiter, or department concerned, reprimanded.

Obviously, it would be impossible to issue all orders to the kitchen or dispense by word of mouth. Utter chaos would result: bills would be wrongly made out, disputes would arise, pilfering on a large scale would take place, and the business would go bankrupt through lack of control. Therefore everything should be checked.

NOTE: There is one exception to this rule. Hotels making inclusive "bed and breakfast" charges do not generally expect waiters to put in checks for breakfast dishes served. It would take too long and waste too many check pads. Control is obtained through the kitchen returns, e.g., 100 visitors—100 breakfasts to be allowed for.

There are two recognised types of checking:

(1) À LA CARTE: Where every dish on the menu is priced separately, so that every check order must state requirement and the price of the dish. These checks are just as important as if cash was passed, and if omitted on the final bill can account for loss of revenue and waiter's "shortages" (short payment).

(2) TABLE D'HÔTE: Where a complete meal or set of courses at a fixed price is charged. Here, no prices need be mentioned, for example, "Room 84, 4 lunches". If the meal deviates from the set menu, the check is expected to show the different dish served, and can be charged extra at the head waiter's discretion.

Making of Checks

Checks should always be written clearly and legibly to avoid mistakes and loss of time. Checks should bear either the room number, or table (house custom), the date, and the waiter's station letter or number.

THE SINGLE CARBON with perforation is used for table d'hôte or à la carte service with direct contact with the kitchen, one copy to kitchen, and one copy on station, or to restaurant cashier (house custom).

THE DOUBLE CARBON is used where two copies are needed
and is almost exclusively for full à la carte restaurants. The
original is generally sent to the kitchen to obtain the goods,
one carbon remains on station, and one carbon copy goes to
restaurant cashier for preparation of the ultimate bill.

THE TRIPLE CARBON. One sheet is of transparent paper
(called a flimsy) so that the waiter has an original and two
copies, to be used as described above. The flimsy remains
either on the guests' table or the side-table, to remind the
commis waiter what is the next course to bring along. This
system is used only in very busy high-class à la carte restaurants where four people at the same table may all order entirely different dishes.

The "Return" Check

For strict control of checking, once a check has been handed
in it cannot be regained. If a commodity has to be returned
for some reason, another check has to be made out marked
"Return" and sent with the dish in order to cancel the trans-
action. These checks should bear the head waiter's signature
to prove their legality to "Control". The waiter thus makes
certain that the item is taken off the bill.

"En Place"

On the table d'hôte a customer sometimes wishes for a slight
change in a dish, so an "En Place" check has to be made—
e.g., "4 Sole frite 'en place' fish du jour". Although no
money is involved, it should be signed by the head waiter to
show that he has permitted the alteration from the standard
menu at no extra charge.

"En Suite"

Also used when serving a table d'hôte meal. In most establishments, the meal order is taken only as far as the main course. When the guest has eaten this dish and the plates have been removed the menu is again presented and the order for the sweet is taken. This check which is headed "en suite" shows the customer's choice as well as room or table number, date and waiter's signature or number.

Extra Charge

Sometimes an extra charge is to be made, so the check could read:—"4 @ 75p. (15/-) Poulet Maryland extra 50p. (10/-)". The waiter must see that the extra charge is placed on the bill.

No Charge (N/C)

Sometimes a waiter requires ingredients from various sources to finish a dish (which has already been charged the full price). As checks are necessary for all items, to cover issue of stock, he makes a check—e.g., "2 Curaçao for Crêpes Suzette N/C", which is duly signed by the head waiter.

Cancellations

In many cases checks have serial numbers and every check must be accounted for, so if a check is spoiled in any way, it has to be cancelled and sent to "Control". The waiter writes "Cancelled" across the check and it is signed by the head waiter. On no account is it to be destroyed or thrown away.

Duplicates

If a check is mislaid, to save the customer waiting another

check can be made, with "Duplicate" written at the top in case the first check gets through to control and the waiter is debited with two orders while only one is charged on the bill. This check requires the head waiter's signature to prevent dishonest usage.

Checking for Wines

To prevent complications and mistakes, wines are usually given a "Bin Number" in the cellar and that number is quoted on the wine list, so the wine waiter orders his wines by the numbers only (see chapter on Wines).

MAKING THE CHECKS. The first figure denotes number and size of bottle, the second figure is the bin number, and, just underneath is the total price (which must be in shillings).

If wines are returned to the cellar for any reason, a return check is made out, with the reason marked on the check ("Unopened", "Corked", etc.), and signed by the person authorised to do so.

```
┌─────────────────────────────────────┐
│                                      │
│                  Table No.           │
│        ────      ─────────           │
│                                      │
│                     15               │
│                                      │
│          1 x 57     140p.            │
│                                      │
│      Date 9/3/70    Sig: W.O.        │
│                                      │
└─────────────────────────────────────┘
```

Checking for Other Drinks

SPIRITS BY MEASURE should be written as numbers of measures and total price—for example, 4 Double Whiskys @

15p. a measure, should read: "8 Whiskys 120p." This method clearly indicates to the cashier how much to charge; saves time and error in making up bills; and prevents friction owing to the possibility of hurried accountancy causing "shortages".

If more than one item is written on the check, the total price should be written in and ringed. Remember—well written, tidy checking avoids most of the shortages which irk the waiting staff.

MINERALS, BEERS, and other open drinks should be checked for in the same way.

Room Number Checking

When guests staying in the hotel take drinks in the lounges or bars, they often prefer to have their orders placed on their "house bill". The waiter then marks the check with the room number and sends a copy to the "bill office". The waiter should politely ask the guest to sign the check—not forgetting to offer a pencil on the plate or salver. This safeguards the guest from drinks being charged unfairly and also safeguards the waiter if the guest queries the amount when he eventually pays. If a guest refuses to sign, the waiter should ask his head waiter to initial the check as a witness against possible dispute.

Tea Shop System

There is another type of control and bill system, used in smaller establishments, tea shops and cafeterias. Here the waiter is entirely responsible for taking his orders, collecting his items, and eventually making out his own bill.

The bill pads have carbon duplicates and may read something like the illustration below. The pads are already printed and cash entries are made only against those items the customer has consumed.

At the end of the service the bill pad is handed to the control and the money paid over. This system has many disadvantages vis-à-vis the restaurant and its control.

Token System

Yet another system—used widely on the Continent, but not very much in England these days—is the "token" or "counter" system.

Here the waiter is supplied with so many counters (chips) on starting duty. For every order taken he puts in an appropriate chip for the item he requires (sandwiches, tea, coffee, beer, etc.). No cash changes hands between the waiter and service. He serves his customers, makes his bills, and on being relieved of his station he pays in to "control" his takings, reckoned on the number of chips he has handed in—less the number of chips still in his possession. This system is very prevalent in beer restaurants in Europe where there are no licensing restrictions and station waiters are on duty for four hours at a stretch.

The Bill

On handing over his station to his relief waiter, he thus leaves everything paid on his station, so that his relief takes over with a clear start. (This really resembles the "change-over" of conductors on the buses, who are responsible for all tickets bought until their reliefs take over.)

Bills are printed with the necessary data, and the waiter or cashier just fills in the general amounts.

The *à la carte* bill usually shows the various courses with a section for wines, beers, minerals, coffee, etc. The bill is made up by totalling the checks for each course and entering the totals in the cash column opposite. Wines should be entered as ordered, but with the amounts now in £ and pence, e.g., 1×57 £1·40.

The *table d'hôte* bill shows at the top the name of the meal with the other items, e.g., wines, beers, etc., underneath.

	£	p.
BREAKFASTS		
4 LUNCHEONS @ 75p.	3	00
DINNERS		
SUPPERS		
WINES 1 x 57	1	40
MINERALS		
SPIRITS	1	20
BEERS		
LIQUEURS		
4 COFFEE		40
SUNDRIES: extra for Chicken		50
Maryland	£6	50
Service 10%		65
W/L Table No. Date.		
A 15 9/3/70 Total	£7	15

Presenting the Bill

For the procedure of presenting the bill to a guest during restaurant service see Chapter 10, pages 130 and 131.

Snack Bar and Counter Service

Although much of what has been written in this book applies to the work of the waiter irrespective of where he is serving, the following instructions are of particular use to those who work in a coffee bar or snack bar, canteen or similar establishment run on a counter-service basis.

The assistant has been referred to as "she" in this chapter but all the instructions apply equally to men assistants.

Preparation—General

The preparation of a counter for service really begins at the end of the previous day's business. There are certain things which must be done immediately after closing time and should never be left to the next day:

All unsold goods should be gathered together and stored in such a way that they may be used the following day. Sandwiches should be covered with a damp muslin cloth, and if possible placed in a tin box to keep them fresh. Pastries should be put away in a *sealed* container in a cool place. Meats, blancmanges and other such articles should be stored in a refrigerator at a temperature of about 38° to 40°F. The bar should be completely cleared of all foodstuffs.

Milk urns should be emptied and filled with water containing a recognised non-caustic detergent liquid or powder, of which there are many efficient ones on the market. This will make it easier to clean the urns the following morning.

The counter and refrigerators should be washed down to remove rougher particles of grease, etc. The floor of the bar in front and behind the counter should be swept ready for washing the next morning.

The main preparation for business is done in the morning, when each assistant is given specific duties to perform. The first essential is to see that cleaning is done thoroughly throughout, beginning from plate glass windows, to mirrors, shelves on walls, milk and ice-cream storage cabinets. The cabinets should be examined each morning and any formation of ice inside the shelves should be carefully removed: this helps to maintain an even temperature and saves electricity.

All foodstuffs stored away the previous night should be put on display and sold before any other, unless their condition has deteriorated.

CLEANING. Shelves should be completely stripped every morning and washed thoroughly with a solution of soap and water. Dust should never be allowed to accumulate.

Refrigerators must be kept scrupulously clean, because if they are dirty they will give off unpleasant smells and, in addition, if the coils (in the case of household refrigerators) or sleeves (in the case of storage cabinets) are regularly cleaned and kept free of grease and ice formation, they will be much more efficient as well as more economical.

Grills should always be kept clean and free of grease. Bread crumbs should be removed carefully in order that no evil-smelling smoke is given off whenever the grills are put into use.

The inside of the urns will need washing, and as they should always be steeped at night the coating of milk inside can be easily removed without damaging the inside by excessive rubbing or scrubbing. Soap and water should be liberally used in washing the outside, so that by rubbing a shiny surface is obtained.

Cutlery, jars, glass, crockery should be examined for any particles of grease or dirt and should always be given a thorough soaking in a solution of water and soda before being used.

ARRANGING CROCKERY AND EQUIPMENT. The best method of arranging crockery, cutlery and glasses depends on the different periods of the day, e.g., if the morning business consists mostly of coffees or teas and pastries (as it usually does), then special attention should be paid to having a good supply of cups, saucers, teaspoons and small plates ready to hand, so that quick service is ensured.

At lunch-time, the bulk of crockery required is of a different nature and this should be prepared ready for use. In the afternoon, the preparations should be made for serving tea, hot and cold drinks, glasses for ice-cream sodas, sundaes and other delicacies, according to the season.

As an interval usually occurs between these busy periods, each assistant should be careful to prepare a "mise en place" during the slack periods.

STACKING AND REMOVING CROCKERY. Crockery should always be stacked where it is most required, e.g., cups and saucers should be placed near coffee and tea urns, soup bowls as near the soup containers as possible, sandwich plates near to the sandwich cases and so on with all other items.

This should be planned in such a way that the least amount of movement is required by each assistant when serving various items on the menu.

The best method of removing crockery is to gather each type (plates, cups, glasses, etc.) separately, and to place them neatly either on trays or wire baskets, in order that when they reach the washing-up department the persons concerned do not have to waste time in sorting them out. Greasy plates should always be kept separate from the others.

Service

METHOD OF REPLENISHING SUPPLIES. Assistants should keep the manager or manageress informed of their requirements before they run out of any commodity. A good assistant will always allow time for supplies of sandwiches and other foodstuffs to be replenished. Various factors have to be considered, such as the season, weather conditions and days of the week. The assistant will know that on a hot day she will require much less cooked foods and much more ice cream, cold drinks, salads and cold sandwiches: she will, therefore, make arrangements accordingly.

KNOWLEDGE OF MENUS, INGREDIENTS, PRICES. All names on the menu should be known by heart and the various ingredients making up the different items on the menu should also be known so that the assistant is never at a loss to explain to a customer any query that may be asked about the menu. Prices should also be noticed and revised continually, for in most bars the assistant who serves also acts as cashier.

TAKING AND CARRYING-OUT ORDERS. An assistant should always address customers politely and in taking an order should say "May I help you, sir?" or "madam?" When an order is given the assistant should repeat it clearly each time in order to avoid mistakes, and when the goods are handed over to the customer the amount to be paid should be clearly stated.

If the customer is hesitant, suggestions as to what type of food and drink is desired should be made. If the customer decides that food is wanted, different items on the menu should be mentioned: stress may be laid on some item that the management particularly wishes to be sold. Once an order is given it should be attended to promptly and efficiently. The customer should be thanked when the order is given and again when payment is made.

CORRECT METHOD OF SERVING. When serving food, bar assistants should always bear in mind that food should never be touched by hand; therefore, when serving sandwiches they should pick them up with sandwich prongs or tongs and place them on the plate.

When hot meals are being served, cutlery should be handed direct to the customer and never thrown on the counter.

Customers should always be warned if the plate is hot, to avoid their being burnt. Salt, pepper and mustard should always be placed close at hand. When serving a dish, it should be held in such a way that fingers do not come into contact with the contents.

Food on a plate should always be served neatly. This applies also to sauces which should never be splashed over the edges of the plate: if by any chance a plate is splashed slightly, it should be carefully wiped with a really clean cloth.

Glasses of hot drinks should always be served on a small plate and customers should be warned if they are likely to be scalded. When serving coffee or tea in cups, the spoon and the handle of the cup should be placed on the right-hand side as it faces the customer. When preparing a drink, whether hot or cold, the cup or tumbler should never be filled to the brim, for this causes inconvenience to the customer as well as splashes.

USE OF CASH REGISTER AND PRACTICE IN GIVING CHANGE. Registers should always be closed after change has been given. Each item should be rung separately. An elementary knowledge of arithmetic is vital, in order that an assistant may be quick in giving correct change.

When a customer pays with a banknote, the *assistant should state the amount she has received as well as the value of the note handed to her.* Change should be given to the customer before the note is inserted in the cash register, so that if the customer should query the change, no doubt can arise as to the value of the note received.

Where there is a shortage of small silver or coppers, the assistant should give change in such a way that she uses up as much large silver as possible.

Foods and Equipment

Although it is not necessary for a waiter or counter assistant to have all the knowledge mentioned under this heading before taking up a post, he (or she) is advised to acquire it during the early part of his career. This can be done by study of more advanced text books and by intelligent application to the work itself.

MAKING UP DRINKS. A knowledge of different types of drinks sold in a bar is of great value to all assistants. The difference between a fruit squash and milkshake syrup is often ignored by the lay person. Very often milk shake syrups are used for making up soda drinks of very poor quality, simply because an assistant does not realise that these syrups were specially manufactured for mixing with milk only.

A general knowledge of the ingredients that go towards making up both squashes and syrups should be acquired, as well as a differentiation between various flavours, simply by tasting. A different taste can soon be acquired, and a diligent assistant should be able to discriminate between good and bad drinks, and should always insist on serving only the good ones. The correct amount of squash or syrup should always be used in making up a drink, as either too small or too big a quantity can easily spoil a perfectly good drink.

CUTTING SANDWICHES. In a busy bar sandwiches are usually prepared behind the scenes, ready for the assistant to serve. However, an assistant should learn how to cut and butter bread and place the right amount of filling to make a wholesome and not uneconomic sandwich. A sense of value should be acquired in the use of the ingredients that go to make up sandwiches.

SERVING BEVERAGES. The equipment behind a bar is varied, and each assistant should have a fairly good knowledge of the component parts of each item, e.g., a knowledge of the temperatures at which hot or cold milk should be kept is essential. Refrigerators used for milk storage have a thermometer set in, which should be carefully watched, and if temperatures rise or fall above or below the set standard the person in charge should be informed at once, so that the fault can be put right.

In snack bars, where milk is a most important ingredient, it is essential that assistants should know the importance of proper milk storage. It is easy for bacteria to multiply rapidly in milk kept in urns that are not strictly hygienic, or in milk poured into containers not properly sterilised. The importance of storing milk in refrigerators immediately it is delivered cannot be stressed enough. All pumps and other equipment used in serving milk should be scrupulously cleaned and sterilised each time they have to be operated.

PREPARING AND SERVING ICE CREAM AND ICE. Ice cream is a very important item in all bars. The temperature at which ice cream is stored affects the service. It is important to serve ice cream which is neither too hard nor too soft. If it is too hard, it slows up service and some of the flavour is lost: if too soft, a lot of waste takes place. Ice cream should be firm but should be easily scooped out when making up various types of ices and sundaes.

It is only with practice that the assistant can gauge the correct temperature at which ice cream should be served.

A knowledge of different types of sundaes, such as Peach Melba, Knickerbocker Glory, Coupe Jacques, Parfait, Banana Split, Mixed Fruit Sundaes, various Nut Sundaes, Chocolate Sundaes, etc., should be acquired by all aspiring bar assistants. The ingredients which go to make up these sundaes should be known, as well as the different standards of ice cream which become apparent only when a person has actually to serve it to the public.

A certain pride is desirable in selling only the very best and an assistant should reach a stage of efficiency when distinction can be made easily between an ice which is really good and one which is of mediocre quality.

Index